This book is dedicated to my zaydah- Joseph Barson
and my son Joseph Barson Shapiro.

Special thanks to Larry Zimmerman,
my first editor and encourager.

# FOR YOUR
# TOMORROWS

## I Give You My Today

F. HOWARD SHAPIRO

CROSSBOOKS

CrossBooks™
A Division of LifeWay
1663 Liberty Drive
Bloomington, IN 47403
www.crossbooks.com
Phone: 1-866-879-0502

© 2014 F. Howard Shapiro. All rights reserved.

No part of this book may be reproduced, stored in a retrieval system, or transmitted by any means without the written permission of the author.

First published by CrossBooks    12/18/2013

ISBN: 978-1-4627-3386-6 (sc)
ISBN: 978-1-4627-3387-3 (hc)
ISBN: 978-1-4627-3385-9 (e)

Library of Congress Control Number: 2013922669

Printed in the United States of America.

This book is printed on acid-free paper.

Any people depicted in stock imagery provided by Thinkstock are models, and such images are being used for illustrative purposes only.
Certain stock imagery © Thinkstock.

Because of the dynamic nature of the Internet, any web addresses or links contained in this book may have changed since publication and may no longer be valid. The views expressed in this work are solely those of the author and do not necessarily reflect the views of the publisher, and the publisher hereby disclaims any responsibility for them.

# CONTENTS

Prologue .................................................................................... xi
Chapter 1 ................................................................................... 1
Chapter 2 ................................................................................... 5
Chapter 3 ................................................................................... 8
Chapter 4 ................................................................................... 11
Chapter 5 ................................................................................... 13
Chapter 6 ................................................................................... 16
Chapter 7 ................................................................................... 18
Chapter 8 ................................................................................... 21
Chapter 9 ................................................................................... 25
Chapter 10 ................................................................................. 31
Chapter 11 ................................................................................. 35
Chapter 12 ................................................................................. 40
Chapter 13 ................................................................................. 42
Chapter 14 ................................................................................. 45
Chapter 15 ................................................................................. 47
Chapter 16 ................................................................................. 51
Chapter 17 ................................................................................. 55
Chapter 18 ................................................................................. 58
Chapter 19 ................................................................................. 61
Chapter 20 ................................................................................. 63
Chapter 21 ................................................................................. 66
Chapter 22 ................................................................................. 70
Chapter 23 ................................................................................. 74

Chapter 24 .................................................................................. 77
Chapter 25 .................................................................................. 81
Chapter 26 .................................................................................. 85
Chapter 27 .................................................................................. 87
Chapter 28 .................................................................................. 89
Chapter 29 .................................................................................. 91
Chapter 30 .................................................................................. 93
Chapter 31 .................................................................................. 95
Chapter 32 .................................................................................. 98
Chapter 33 ................................................................................ 100
Chapter 34 ................................................................................ 104
Chapter 35 ................................................................................ 110
Chapter 36 ................................................................................ 114
Chapter 37 ................................................................................ 116
Chapter 38 ................................................................................ 119
Chapter 39 ................................................................................ 121
Chapter 40 ................................................................................ 122
Chapter 41 ................................................................................ 127
Chapter 42 ................................................................................ 129
Chapter 43 ................................................................................ 133
Chapter 44 ................................................................................ 135
Chapter 45 ................................................................................ 137
Epilogue .................................................................................... 141

# For Your Tomorrows
(I Give you My Today)

### *Overture*

*But you don't have to be in a hurry.*
*You're not running from anybody!*
*GOD is leading you out of here,*
*And the God of Israel is also your rear guard.*
*Just watch my servant blossom!*
*Exalted, tall, head and shoulders above the crowd!*
*But he didn't begin that way.*
*At first everyone was appalled.*
*He didn't even look human -*
*A ruined face, disfigured past recognition.*
*Nations all over the world will be in awe, taken aback.*
*Kings shocked into silence when they see him.*
*For what was unheard of they'll see with their own eyes,*
*What was unthinkable they'll have right before them.*

*Isaiah 52:12-15 (The Message)*


*For I know the plans I have for you, declares the LORD. Plans for welfare and not for evil, to give you a future and a hope.*

*Jeremiah 29:11 (ESV)*


*"In the end I will turn things around for the people.*
*I'll give them a language undistorted, unpolluted.*
*Words to address GOD in worship and, united to serve me*
*With their shoulders to the wheel.*
*All my scattered, exiled people will come home with offerings for worship.*

*You'll no longer have to be ashamed of all those acts of rebellion.*
*I'll leave a core of people among you who are poor in spirit.*
*They'll make their home in GOD.*
*Your GOD is present among you,*
*A strong Warrior there to save you.*
*Happy to have you back.*
*He'll calm you with his love and delight you with his songs.*
*The accumulated sorrows of your exile will dissipate.*
*I, your God, will get rid of them for you.*
*You've carried those burdens long enough.*
*I'll get rid of all those who've made your life miserable.*
*I'll heal the maimed; I'll bring home the homeless.*
*You'll be famous and honored all over the world.*
*You'll see it with your own eyes—all those painful partings*
*Turned into reunions!*

Zephaniah 3: 9-20 (The Message)

*My God, why have you forsaken me?*
*Why are you so far from saving me?*
*I cry by day, but you do not answer, and by night, but I find no rest.*
*In you my Zaydah's trusted; he trusted,*
*And you delivered them.*
*To you he cried and was rescued,*
*In you he trusted and were not put to shame. But I am a worm and not a man, scorned by mankind and despised by the people.*
*Yet you are he who took me from the womb; you made me trust you at my mother's breasts. Be not far from me, for trouble is near, and there is none to help.*
*O LORD, do not be far off!*

*O you, my help, come quickly to my aid!*
*I will tell of your name to my brothers.*
*In the midst of the congregation, I will praise you:*
*For God has not despised or abhorred*
*The affliction of the afflicted,*
*And he has not hidden his face from him,*
*But has heard, when he cried to him.*
*The afflicted shall eat and be satisfied.*
*Those who seek him shall praise the LORD!*
*May your hearts live forever!*
*All the ends of the earth shall remember and*
*Turn to the LORD, and all the families of the earth*
*Shall worship before you.*

*Psalm 22 (ESV)*

# PROLOGUE

These scriptures remind me that God has a purpose, a dream, a goal and, more importantly, God never stops pursuing His dreams. God believes in us. God loves us as we are. God loves our enemies. This book is not about a God who focuses on simply forgiving sinners and providing us tickets to Heaven. This book is about a God who focuses on tenderly searching for us and including us in His Kingdom plans now. If Heaven is also part of His plan as well, Hallelujah? God, the central character of this book, possesses an extraordinary love for us! If you feel far from God, don't despair. He is searching for you. God doesn't give up until all that was lost is found.

Some of you are going to read this memoir and question my story.

You will analyze, pick apart, criticize, and point out the incidents that are just too fantastic to believe. Maybe it's because you have never let yourself believe in or do anything fantastic. Maybe in the process of believing in or doing something fantastic, you have been burned and disappointed. Maybe it's because your fear of failure has frustrated your facility to feel and live with something prodigious.

I invite you to analyze, pick apart, criticize, and point out the incidents that seem just too fantastic to believe. I invite you to think about them, because you may recognize the fantastic things in your own life and give belated thanks to a God who has never condemned us for our mistakes and imperfections. As a matter of fact, in my story, my sins and mistakes reveal more about God than my righteousness. The bottom line of my story is that it's only in darkness that we see the brightest light.

I'm not trying to make a theological statement about God, even though I understand that any word spoken about God is in some sense a theological statement. I am simply trying to tell my story with God as the central character. The truth be known, I no longer think very much about my theological position; I think a lot more about my story.

My story really begins before I even knew it. My story is that God took an interest in me before I was even born.

This was also Jeremiah's story.

*"Before I formed you in the womb I knew you, and before you were born I consecrated you; I appointed you a prophet to the nations." Then I said, "Ah, Lord GOD! Behold, I do not know how to speak, for I am only a youth." But the LORD said to me, "Do not say, I am only a youth, for to all to whom I send you, you shall go, and whatever I command you, you shall speak. Do not be afraid of them, for I am with you to deliver you says the LORD."*[1]

---

[1] Jeremiah 1:5-8

# CHAPTER 1

*While they were being quickly heated, he commanded his executioners to cut out the tongue of the one who had spoken for the others, to scalp him and cut off his hands and feet, while the rest of his brothers and his mother looked on.*[2]

Before you can begin to really picture the "today" that I offer for your "tomorrow", I need to paint two pictures of yesterday: one of a Haverhill Massachusetts heroine and one of a Christian hero. Both of yesterday's images influence how I live out my today.

Thomas and Hannah Dustin and their nine children lived on a farm in Haverhill. When their farm was attacked by the Abenaki Indians in 1697, Thomas fled with eight of their children. Hannah, her newborn daughter Martha, and her nurse Mary Neff were captured and forced to march into the wilderness. While on the journey to the Abenaki camp,

---

[2] Second Maccabees 7: 4. Maccabees is a deuterocanonical book which focuses on the Jews' revolt against Antiochus IV Epiphanies and concludes with the defeat of the Syrian general Nicanor in 161 BC by Judas Maccabeus, the hero of the work. Catholics and Orthodox consider the work to be canonical and part of the Bible. Protestants and Jews reject most of the doctrinal innovations present in the work. The story of Hanukkah (the 8-day Jewish festival that is usually celebrated in December is preserved in the books of the First and Second Maccabees.

Hannah Dustin reported that the Abenaki killed the six-day-old Martha by smashing her against a tree.

Three weeks later, Hannah Dustin escaped Abenaki captivity by using a tomahawk to scalp one man, two women, and two children while they slept. Upon her return, she went to Boston to petition the General Court of Massachusetts Bay for bounty money on their scalps.

While in Boston, Hannah told her story to Reverend Cotton Mather, who saw her escape as a modern miracle and recorded it in his Magnalia Christi Americana. Mather's account spurred the moral and social questions to which writers such as John Greenleaf Whittier, Nathaniel Hawthorne, and Henry David Thoreau would later respond: Is killing one's Indian captors justified? Is killing Indian women and children justifiable? Is killing Catholic Indians justifiable? Is scalping Indian victims and collecting a bounty on their scalps justifiable?

In Haverhill, Hannah Dustin's story continues to encourage the community, although the scalped heads of the Indians have been removed from the monument. I recently drove by the statue, and Hannah looks really furious that someone taken has her scalps.

Along with the monument in Grand Army Park (GAR) Park inspiring Haverhill's homeless, destitute, and drug dealers, Hannah Dustin is remembered by the Hannah Dustin Health Care Center, the Hannah Dustin Rest Home, the Hannah Dustin Elementary School, and a Hannah Dustin bobble head doll. The doll has the inscription "A Mother's Revenge." It is sold at the John Greenleaf Whittier birthplace and the Haverhill Public Library.

Not everyone sees what the Reverend Cotton Mather sees in Hannah Dustin's story. Some see her legend as racist and one that glorifies violence. Margaret Bruchak notes that Hannah Dustin's story contradicts the Abenaki view of combat and captivity:

> *The whole point of taking a captive was to transport that person safely to their camp. For the whole of that*

*journey, they were treated like family. When captives were taken, they were almost immediately handed off from the warriors to individuals who would then look after them. Hannah, we know for a fact, was handed over to an extended family group of two adult men, three women, seven children and one white child. It wasn't when she was in the midst of warfare that she did these supposedly brave acts. It was when she was in the care of a family. If she had merely escaped, there probably would be very little story to tell, but the fact that she escaped, then stopped and went back to collect scalps* – the bloody-mindlessness of it is really quite remarkable.³

While Haverhill erected statues of Hannah Dustin scalping Indians, Germany erected statues of Martin Luther killing Jews. When I was 10 years old, Morris Strassburg, my Hebrew School teacher introduced me to Martin Luther, the seminal figure of the Protestant Reformation. In 1543, Martin Luther reached much of Europe with *On the Jews and Their Lies* in which he pronounced that the Jews are a "base, whoring people, full of the devil's dung . . . which they wallow in like swine."⁴ He also seemed to advocate their murder, writing, "We are at fault in not slaying them."⁵

Although Luther did not invent the term anti-Jewish, he certainly promoted it to a level never before seen in Europe. Four hundred years after it was written, Luther's sentiments were preached by Adolf Hitler during the Nuremberg rallies.

---

3 Hannah Dustin: The Judgment of History By Kathryn Whitford Associate Professor, Department of English, University of Wisconsin-Milwaukee
4 Obermann, Heiko. Luthers Werke. Erlangen 1854, 32:282, 298, cited in Michael, Robert. Holy Hatred: Christianity, Antisemitism, and the Holocaust. New York: Palgrave Macmillan, 2006, p. 113.
5 Luther, Martin. On the Jews and Their Lies 343-344

*My feelings as a Christian point me to my Lord and Savior as a fighter. They point me to the man who once in loneliness, surrounded only by a few followers, recognized these Jews for what they were and summoned men to fight against them. Today, I recognize more profoundly than ever before, that it was for this, that He had to shed his blood upon the Cross.*[6]

Ultimately, whether Hannah Dustin and Martin Luther are heroes or villains is a matter of perspective. Either way, both appear to be archetypes of the virtuous person who acts violently and still remains innocent. Whether heroes or villains, their violent actions have contributed to the fears, anger, doubts, and lusts that are part of the day that I am offering you. Indeed, sometimes I remember so much about yesterday that I still find it hard to recognize what God does today and promises to do tomorrow.

As I think about Mr. Strassburg, I am mindful that although he was my teacher for three years, I only remember two things about him. First and foremost, I remember him seething with anger as he recounted Luther's anti-Semitism. However when I dig a little deeper, I also remember that he ended his rant against Luther with an afterthought, "Do not judge Christianity by people like Martin Luther, Christianity also gave us St. Francis of Assisi, one of the most wonderful persons that ever lived." In retrospection, Mr. Strassburg's profound admiration for St. Francis somehow must have stimulated my own calling- a calling that at one time almost included the Franciscan Order. But before I met Francis of Assisi, I met Bobby of Haverhill.

---

[6] Adolf Hitler: A speech delivered April 12, 1922, published in "My New Order,"

# CHAPTER 2

*I found one day in school, a boy of medium size ill-treating a smaller boy. I expostulated, but he replied, "The bigs hit me, so I hit the babies – that's fair." In these words, he epitomized the history of the human race.*[7]

*Everyone who wants to do good to the human race always ends up in universal bullying.*[8]

My first terrible memory was of anti-Jewish ravings.

I was a fat Jewish kid who lisped and the only Jewish kid in the Tilton School. Everyone in the neighborhood knew that my father had abandoned my family when I was eighteen months old.

One day on my way home from Mrs. Kozub's fourth grade class, I met some kids coming home from Catechism with Bibles in their hands.

"Hey, it's the fat, fatherless, lisping kike who reads real good. I wonder if he can read this. I'm not a good enough reader."

Bobby Mozzolla pushed a Bible into my hands and told me to read. So I read, *"Pilate took Jesus and had him scourged. The soldiers wove a crown out of thorns and placed it on his head, and clothed him in a*

---

[7]   Bertrand Russell
[8]   Aldous Huxley

*purple cloak, and shouted, 'Hail, King of the Jews!' And they struck him repeatedly."*

As soon as I finished reading, they raised lead pipes and branches mirroring the monument of Hannah Dustin raising her tomahawk. As they beat me, my eyes felt as if they were bleeding.

As I cried, Bobby yelled, "This is for killing Jesus!"

I screamed through the tears, "How could I have killed Jesus!"

Someone sneered, "I wanna hear the fat kike read St. Matthew."

*I read, "The chief priests and the elders persuaded the crowds to ask for Barabbas and destroy Jesus."*

The beatings continued (both Jesus and mine) and I continued to read:

> *Pilate said to them, "Then what shall I do with the Jesus called Messiah?" They said, "Let him be crucified!" But he said, "Why? What evil has he done?" They shouted louder, "Let him be crucified!" Pilate took water and washed his hands saying, "I am innocent of this man's blood. Look to it yourselves." The Jews said "His blood be upon us and our children.*

Mrs. Kozub found me lying in a pool of Jesus' blood. She suggested to my mother that perhaps we should move to a different school district.

That summer we moved to Main Street. I was now able to go to school with other Jewish kids. My teacher was even Jewish. As I walked into Mrs. Hirschfield's class, I heard someone say "Just what we need, one more fat, fatherless, lisping kike." It was Bobby Mozzolla. He had moved to Main Street, too. I felt as if I had died and gone to an eternal hell.

As he jabbed me in the chest, I heard him threaten, "Give me a quarter or buy me lunch." Most of the time I gave in, knowing what would happen if I didn't. I hadn't fully healed from the beating on the street six months earlier, but that was nothing compared to the beatings I had suffered inside John Greenleaf Whittier School. I can still feel Bobby and his friends slamming my head against the locker. My head was a mere eggshell in their hands. Teachers learned not to make a big deal about my two black eyes and the blood stains on my torn shirts.

My worst experience was in Mr. Backus's sixth grade class. I sat next to my friend Jimmy. One day his pen leaked on his desk and somehow on my shirt. Jimmy's gasp was only heard by Bobby who got up, grabbed a paper towel from the dispenser at the back of the room, and began rubbing the inkblot all over my shirt. He then picked up Jimmy's leaky pen and began rubbing it against my white pants.

Bobby laughed and the class looked back at us and began to laugh—even Jimmy and Mr. Backus laughed. I knew then that bullying was a way of life for Bobby and his friends. It was a rite of passage – a rite that I thought would have killed me.

I didn't go to school much after that. For the next seven years, I faked every sickness that I could think of to avoid contact with Bobby Mozzolla and my former friend Jimmy. My grades suffered. The principals and guidance counselors would call the house and sometimes even visit, but I wasn't going to allow myself to get beaten. I do have one wonderful memory from Whittier School, it was a fifth grade field trip to the Haverhill Historical Museum.

# CHAPTER 3

*Fill up my cup Mazel tov*
*Look at her dancing, just take it off"*[9]

Have you ever had a moment when suddenly, unexpectedly, you knew more than you were supposed to know, and as a result, you were at peace with yourself and the universe? Jewish mystics connect this feeling to mazel. *"Mazel"* is the root of the soul – the presence of God that shines down on us. Mazel tov means far more than the Black Eyed Peas imagined. Mazel literally means "a drip from above."

When you say "mazel tov" to someone, you are pronouncing this profound blessing: *"May this drip of inspiration from your soul above not dissolve, but have a lasting effect, that as a result of this event, you live life with higher consciousness."*

*Follow your heart, your intuition.*
*It will lead you in the right direction.*
*Let go of your mind.*
*Your intuition is easy to find.*
*Just follow your heart, baby.*[10]

---

[9] The Black Eyed Peas: "I've Got A Feeling"
[10] Jewel – "Intuition"

When I was ten years old, I let go of my mind, followed my heart, and discovered mazel. Judy Weissman sat next to Bobby Mozzolla in Mrs. Hirschfield's class. Judy had just moved to Haverhill, and her father had just become the new executive director of the temple. She was brilliant and lovely. I rushed to sit next to her at the Haverhill Historical Museum.

At some point after looking at artifacts like Hannah Dustin's tomahawk, the museum curator asked, "Who knows how many states were in the Union at the start of the Civil War? If you're not sure, try picturing the first Union flag, count the stars and there's the answer."

I was only ten and had no conscious idea of what the first Union flag looked like, but a flag appeared in my mind's eye and I slowly counted the stars. I'm not sure how long it took, because the curator had already changed the subject.

I raised my hand and said, "In the Union there were thirty-three states at the start of the Civil War."

"No one has ever gotten that right before, you must be a genius," the curator replied.

I knew I wasn't a genius, but the creator of mazel wanted Judy Weissman to be impressed, and she was.

Fifty-two years later, I mentioned this incident to a friend, and he was certain there were more than thirty-three stars on the Union flag. I Googled the Union flag and I saw flags with thirty-four, thirty-five, and thirty-six stars. Had I miscounted? Had the curator been wrong?

Then I saw a picture of the Fort Sumter flag, lowered by Major Robert Anderson on April 14, 1861 in Charleston, South Carolina, three days after the outset of the Civil War.[11] That flag had thirty-three stars. On April 14, 1865, four years to the day after the surrender, and as part of a celebration of the Union victory, Anderson raised the same Fort Sumter

---

[11] By the way, my stepson just moved to Charleston – a coincidence?

flag in triumph over the battered remains of the fort. The same flag that raised my triumph at the Whittier School.

Later that night, President Lincoln was shot at Ford's Theater. Some might say that his mazel had run out. I'm convinced that his true mazel was finally revealed. It's only in darkness that we see the greatest light. Before the Black Eyed Peas wished us mazel tov, my grandmother Bobe used to sing:

*You got to have some mazel*
*Mazel means good luck*
*And with a little mazel*
*You never will get stuck*

# CHAPTER 4

*Greece and the islands in the Aegean Sea have given birth to many myths and legends of war and adventure. In addition, these once-proud stones, these ruined and shattered temples, bear witness to the civilization that flourished, then died and to the demigods and heroes who inspired those legends on this sea and these islands. However, though the stage is the same, ours is a legend of our own times, and its heroes are not demigods, but ordinary people. In 1943, so the story goes, 2000 years later.*[12]

In the Jewish community, you need more than just mazel, you need a tzadik. A tzadik is a profoundly righteous man – a spiritual master, a hero, a rescuer. Josel (Joseph) of Rosheim was a tzadik. As a Shtadlan (Court Jew), he dedicated himself to intervening with various rulers to save the lives of German Jews. He even managed to publish a defense against the attacks of Martin Luther that subsequently blocked anti-Jewish legislation and saved many Jews against charges of ritual murder.

Four centuries later, my grandfather Josel (Joseph) Barson was my tzadik. He seemed to dedicate himself to intervening with both my family and the universe on my behalf. He alone was my guardian and savior.

---

[12] The introduction to the film "Guns of Naverone" – 1961

When I won two tickets on the radio to see *The Guns of Navarone*[13] at the Colonial Theatre, he was the only one I wanted to go with.

When Zaydah[14] and I got to the Colonial Theatre, he hesitated and said, "Freddie, I'm sorry but I don't think I can go."

When I asked him why, he said, "I need to visit Louis Fleisher."

"Zaydah, I'll just go with you. I wanna be with you."

He smiled saying, "You take the ticket, and if I get back in time, I'll meet you."

I put the ticket in his hand, "No Zaydah, kids get in for twenty cents but it costs $1.00 for adults. You take the ticket and please come back."

He left and I reluctantly went in alone. I sat with some kids but it wasn't the same. I sat through the cartoons, the newsreels and then the feature movie started. Just as the credits came on, a small elderly man made his way down the darkened aisle. It was Zaydah. I ran into the aisle, hugged him, kissed him, and knew that all was right with the world.

Later, Mom told me that Zaydah didn't visit Louis Fleisher. Elders of the synagogue had found out he was going to a movie on Shabbat and were ready to discipline him. According to my mom, he told them, "Being with my grandson is more important than obeying the tradition."

My definition of a tzadik is someone who can destroy seemingly impregnable forces and make everything all right with the world. Zaydah died two years later. My last memory of him was taking him to the men's room before my Bar Mitzvah. I was late for my Bar Mitzvah, but it was the least I could do for a tzadik. Zaydah was seventy-six years old and very tired of life. I was thirteen, and I was tired of life also.

---

[13] The film or the book retells the story of an Allied commando team's efforts to destroy a seemingly impregnable German fortress in the Aegean Sea that prevented 2,000 troops from being rescued.
[14] A Jewish term of endearment for grandfather.

# CHAPTER 5

*You want so bad to leave that whirlwind storm*
*But you can't find no place to grab on*
*Round and round you go again*
*And it just ain't easy, Lord*[15]

*God has never resorted to using any kind of vessel that isn't filled with the Holy Ghost. He doesn't have to borrow vessels from anyone else; He can make His own vessels, clean them up, sanctify them, and get them ready for His use. And if God is going to use man, He is going to use him in such a way that the Spirit of God can operate through him. Man won't do the work, but the Spirit and power of the Holy Ghost will do it through man. I have often said, "It isn't my hand that heals the sick or performs a miracle, it's the Spirit of God and the gift and power of God working through a man that is yielded to Him."*[16]

Zaydah had been dead three months, and I really needed a tzadik. One Sunday morning I was getting dressed to go to the temple when I heard an insane man on the TV scream, "Some of you need a miracle today. Stand up, place your hand on your television, and ask Jesus for a sign, 'Jesus prove to me that you are the Son of God, do this for me.'"

---

[15]  The Allman Brothers "Just Ain't easy"
[16]  The Reverend A.A. Allen

I thought back to Bobby Mozzolla and the others who had bullied me with their Bibles. I felt a thousand needles piercing my soul. Oh, I stood up all right. I placed my hand on the TV and I swore at Jesus and then found myself adding, *OK Jesus, prove to me that you're more than the faker I think you are. I've been looking for my Channel Master 6 transistor radio – find it for me.* Before I knew it, the phone rang.

An angry, old man's voice asked, "Is this the kid that shovels the snow from my driveway?"

"Yes."

"The last time you were here you left something on the telephone post, you better get it before it freezes!"

I immediately knew that it was my radio. Jesus had found it.

What I didn't know is that A. A. Allen, the insane man on TV, was considered by many to be a fake. By 1963, he had been arrested several times, jumped bail, and subsequently left the Assemblies of God churches.[17] I also didn't know about the goon squads he reportedly hired to rough up reporters who showed up for his revivals with a notepad or camera.

I also didn't know that he supposedly provided wheelchairs for those who were tired of standing in a healing line for hours, and that when he got to them, he'd pull them out of the wheelchairs and declared them healed. Those watching the scene on TV assumed that the followers who were waiting in line had come to the revival in wheelchairs.

I did know that ten years later, A. A. Allen was found dead in the Jack Tar Hotel in San Francisco after a drinking binge. Of course, none of

---

[17] With approximately 57 to 60 million adherents, the Assemblies of God is the sixth largest Christian denomination. The Assemblies originated from the Pentecostal revival of the early 20th century and believe in the Pentecostal distinctive of baptism with the Holy Spirit with the evidence of speaking in tongues.

that has ever mattered. That Sunday morning in 1964, I sensed that Jesus was some kind of Savior. It's not easy for a Jewish eighth grader to trust in Jesus; my only hope was that Haverhill High school would be salvific.

Why did I assume that in high school the beatings would stop? Why did I assume that Bobby Mozzolla would move, be sent to reform school[18], or die before September 1964? Maybe it's because Haverhill had just built a new high school, and it was no longer located across the street from the statue of Hannah Dustin and the scalped Indians.

---

[18] Reform school was essentially penal institutions for teenage boys who had gotten into serious trouble with the law. Today, no state openly or officially refers to its juvenile correctional institutions as "reform schools," although such institutions still exist.

# CHAPTER 6

*The teacher dressed impeccably, had a radiant smile, and spoke professionally. It's horrible to say this, but if you can pull off those three simple things, the bureaucrats will be dazzled and they will let you keep your job -- even if you belong in jail.*[19]

Bobby Mozzolla had many friends at Haverhill High, and it didn't take long for every bully to see me as an easy way of achieving their rite of passage. I was punched, pushed, shoved, kicked, threatened, ganged up on, and stolen from. Those who did not want to hurt me physically, spread awful rumors about me, excluded me from their cliques, teased me, and provoked others to gang up on me.

My bullies included my teacher, Mr. C. At a Parent and Teacher meeting, he told my mom that I was inattentive and that I couldn't seem to focus. He was right; I chose to look out the window and gaze at the trees rather than look at him and gain his attention. Whenever he saw me looking at him, he would somehow find a reason to ridicule me. One day, I asked to go to the restroom. When I returned to class, the door was locked. I saw and heard Mr. C. and students laughing.

During my freshmen and sophomore years, I did everything I could to miss school. Subsequently, I flunked subjects like Algebra, Geometry,

---

[19] Velma Konwea

Chemistry, and any other class that required regular attendance in order to pass.

In my junior year, I met my Savior – Ed Johnson, a local DJ who was also my public speaking teacher. His belief and faith in me inspired me to want to be a deejay. My most memorable high school moment was during an assigned school project when I got to interview the host of WBZ's Subway-Dick Summer[20], music icon Al Kooper and several Boston musicians, including Bruce Arnold, the leader of Orpheus.

Based on Mr. Johnson's recommendation, I received a scholarship to Grahm Junior College, a Boston college that had a strong communications program. I wasn't bullied by students or teachers in that college. One professor even took me under his wing and introduced me to a new book that had just been published *The Satanic Bible*.

---

[20] WBZ's Dick Summer was one of Boston's most popular disc jockeys during the 1960's. His overnight show was heard in 38 states and up in parts of Canada. His Sunday 8-11pm show "The Subway" featured lesser known but upcoming artists from the Boston area as well as other nationally known singers. He was among the first to play the music of Boston groups like Orpheus, Ultimate Spinach, The Beacon Street Union and The J Geils Band

# CHAPTER 7

*When all religious faith in lies has waned, it is because man has become closer to himself and farther from God; closer to the Devil.*[21]

*The Satanic Bible* by Anton LaVey is a series of reflections and rituals about Satanism. The book has been called the most important document to influence contemporary Satanism.[22]

LaVey saw himself as an atheistic Satanist. He claimed to not believe in the existence of God, but saw God as a projection that we create.

Although LaVey Satanists do not believe in the existence of a personal God or Devil, more traditional Satanist groups (often referred to as true or real Satanists) recognize LaVey's work as influential. Many Satanists attribute their conversions or discoveries of Satanism to *The Satanic Bible*, with 20 percent of respondents to a survey by James Lewis mentioning that Bible as a direct influence on their conversion.[23]

---

[21] Anton LaVey
[22] Legitimating New Religions. Page 16. New Brunswick, NJ, USA: Rutgers University Press.
[23] ibid Page 117

My belief in God kept me from pursuing Satanism, but LaVey's book influenced me. It helped me recognize that we all have a carnal side to us that no amount of praying can eradicate. After only one semester, my search for ways to blend my belief in God with my own carnality resulted in my suspension from college. That summer I went to Woodstock, totaled my car on the way home, began doing drugs, and tried to kill myself twice. One day I heard Bobe say, "Sarah why don't you just kill him?"

My mom cried, "Because I don't want to go to jail."

I was used to Bobe's anger but not to my mom's tears.

Half an hour later, male voices merged into the melee, and I knew that I would be threatened by a well-meaning yet unenlightened bully that Bobe had commissioned. As I left the house, I heard a Bob Dylan song on my Channel Master. Dylan wrote the song when a hotel clerk thought he looked like a deadbeat and refused to give him a room until Joan Baez vouched for his good character. Would anyone ever vouch for my good character? Would Pharaoh and Goliath ever be put in their place?

*Oh, the fishes will laugh*
*As they swim out of the path,*
*And the sea gulls, they'll be smilin'*
*While the rocks on the sand*
*will proudly stand . . .*
*The hour that the ship comes in.*

*A song will lift,*
*As the main sail shifts*
*The ship on to the shoreline*
*And the sun all respect*
*Every face on the deck,*
*The hour that the ship comes in.*

*Oh, the foes will rise with the sleep still in their eyes' Then they'll raise their hands saying "We'll meet all your demands!"*

*But like Pharaohs' tribe they'll all be drowned in the tide' And Like Goliath, they'll be conquered. The hour the ship comes in.*[24]

---

[24]  Bob Dylan: When My Ship Comes In

# CHAPTER 8

In the 1970's, no one blended belief in God and belief in carnality better than Robert DeGrimston de Grimston and Mary Ann McClean MacLean, founders of the Process Church of the Final Judgment.

In 1963, Robert de Grimston and Mary Ann MacLean met at the L. Ron Hubbard Institute of Scientology in London. De Grimston was tall, handsome, charismatic, and emotionally dependent— a perfect match for Mary Ann who had been abandoned at an early age. She emigrated to the USA, made her living as a prostitute, briefly married welterweight and middleweight boxing champion Sugar Ray Robinson. When she moved back to London after divorcing him, she set up a high-class call girl service. Mary Ann MacLean knew how to exploit people.

Robert was too intelligent and Mary Ann too self-willed to follow L. Ron Hubbard. When members of their Scientology group inherited a lot of money, Robert and Mary Ann convinced them to donate the money to their movement named The Process. In 1966, in search of a sanctuary, thirty Processeans traveled to the coastal village of Sisal on the Yucatán Peninsula and discovered Xtul, a place of ruins. In Mayan, Xtul is translated as "end." For the Process, it was only the beginning.

The Processeans set up camp in an abandoned salt factory. For them, Xtul was an Eden-like paradise. Unfortunately, the paradise was lost when Hurricane Inez visited them for three days and destroyed much of the peninsula. De Grimston saw it as a rite of passage. They had experienced paradise and now they had experienced Satan. De Grimston had met the twin Gods of Love and Violence. Process theology was formed and written as *The Xtul Dialogues*, which elucidates that there are three forces or gods that rule human existence: Jehovah, Satan, and Lucifer.

These three gods represent the three basic human patterns of reality:

- Jehovah, a wrathful god of vengeance who demands discipline, courage, ruthlessness, and dedication to duty, purity, and self-denial.
- Lucifer, the Light Bearer, urges us to enjoy life and success, while practicing gentleness, kindness, and peace with one another. Our human inability to value success without descending into greed, jealousy, and self-importance has brought Lucifer into disrepute. He now has become mistakenly identified with Satan.
- Satan instills in his followers two directly opposite qualities: an urge to rise above our physical appetites, to become all soul and no body; a desire to wallow in a morass of violence, lunacy, and excessive physical indulgence. Humans fear the latter of Satan's nature, which is why Satan is seen as God's adversary.

According to *The Xtul Dialogues*, to varying degrees, these God-patterns exist in all of us, and Christ will ultimately meld the personalities of Jehovah, Satan, and Lucifer.[25]

De Grimston realized that his mission was to return to London and preach the word of their imminent apocalyptic unification. When he returned to London, however, the Processeans were greeted by

---

[25] Please do not confuse the theology set forth in the Xtul Dialogues with traditional Process theology that posits that God is always changing, as is the universe, thus our knowledge of God must be progressing as we learn more about him. Famous process theologians and philosophers include Alfred North Whitehead, Charles Hartshorne, Henry Nelson Wieman, and John B. Cobb, Jr. Another famous theologian whose work paralleled the process theology movement was Pierre Teilhard de Chardin, a Jesuit priest and biologist

newspapers describing them as "Mind Benders." Undeterred, they opened a 24-hour coffee bar called Satan's Cave and began wearing black capes, turtle necks, and shiny silver crosses that had a serpent wrapped around it. This was the uniform Robert de Grimston was wearing in their food kitchen in Cambridge, Massachusetts, the night I met him.

I was captivated by his sermon on Matthew 5: 44-8.

> *You have heard that it was said, 'Love your neighbor and hate your enemy.' But I tell you, love your enemies and pray for those who persecute you, that you may be children of your Father in heaven. He causes his sun to rise on the evil and the good, and sends rain on the righteous and the unrighteous. If you love those who love you, what reward will you get? Are not even the tax collectors doing that? And if you greet only your own people, what are you doing more than others are? Do not even pagans do that? Be perfect, therefore, as your heavenly Father is perfect.*

De Grimston explained that if "loving your enemy" is the prime rule of behavior, then the goal of the Process is to love Satan without loving his evil acts. I thought back to Hannah Dustin using a tomahawk to kill Catholic Indians, Martin Luther using threats to share his gospel, and Bobby Mozzolla preaching with a lead pipe. It made sense that God and Satan are in this thing together. Somehow, both contribute to our lives. De Grimston said that I needed to see Christ as judge and Satan as executioner of Christ's judgments. I understood that. I needed to worship God while loving Satan.

Next Saturday at 7:00 p.m., I was ready to become an acolyte in the Process Church. After de Grimston's message, an elder took me upstairs into a room that had a Christian cross on one wall and a goat's head in a pentagram on another. In the center of the room was an altar of candles pointing in the four cardinal directions that symbolized their unity with all of creation. Frankincense was burned in the center, showing Christ as the heart of the Process. We sat on cushions in a circle around the altar as music played behind us.

As Robert de Grimston smiled at me, fear smashed me in the face at the speed of light. I needed to leave. I told the elder I was afraid that something had happened to my car and that I needed to check it. He cackled at my fear and didn't want me to leave but finally agreed to accompany me. I told him the car was parked at least three blocks away, but he insisted on staying with me. We got to the car and I discovered that my car *had* been broken into. Someone had stolen my 8-track player and all of my Grateful Dead 8-track cartridges. The elder told me that this was Karma. God, however, told me that this was a warning and to leave. As I left, the elder warned me that not going through the acolyte, Process would release more bad Karma than I had ever experienced before.

In 1974, Robert and Mary Ann ran out of Karma and divorced. Mary Ann renounced de Grimston's theology of the unity between God and Satan and renamed the church the Foundation Faith of the Millennium. Today the church is called Best Friends Animal Society and is one of the best known animal sanctuaries in the world. Mary Ann lived at the sanctuary in Utah with her husband Gabriel de Peyer. Robert de Grimston became a business consultant in Manhattan.

Vincent Bugliosi, the prosecutor in the Charles Manson family trial, comments in his book *Helter Skelter* that there may be evidence that Manson borrowed philosophically from the Process Church. He says that representatives of the church visited Manson in jail after his arrest. There is no strong evidence of any connection between the Process Church and the Manson family; however, I have a considerable connection to Charles Manson.

# CHAPTER 9

*Never thought about tomorrow*
*Seemed like a long time to come*
*How could I be so blind?*
*Not to see you were the one*
*I must've got lost somewhere down the line.*[26]

In 1969, when I needed to talk to anyone about anything deeper than a nick, I'd visit Tony Saulnier. Three months earlier, Tony had introduced me to his friend Lynn. As the three of us listened to Frank Zappa's recording of "Happy Together" from *Live at the Fillmore East*, Lynn embarrassingly laughed and confessed, "When I was a teenager, I used to sit cross-legged on the floor and sing that song to my rosary."

Tony laughed and said, "If you think that's crazy, check out who Lynn knows."

Lynn proceeded to tell me about her high school friend Linda Drouin with whom she used to double-date -. Linda Drouin was a shy, smart, "starry-eyed romantic" who ended up dropping out of Wilton High School and leaving home at the age of sixteen due to problems with her stepfather. She headed out west looking for God. Instead, she got

---

[26] "I Must've Got Lost", The J. Geils Band, Songwriter Seth Justman and Peter Wolf.

married, pregnant, divorced, and married again to Robert Kasabian. Through her husband, Linda Kasabian met Charles Manson.

When I left the Processeans in Harvard Square on June 27, 1971, I drove to Tony Saulnier's White Street apartment where the topic du jour quickly became "How do you change your Karma?" Tony finally laughed and said, "The only way I know how to change Karma is to simply do something about it." Then he asked, "What is the biggest change you could possibly make in your life?"

I blurted out, "Changing how I feel about my dad."

Tony suggested that I set out to Chicago, find him, and change things. He also strongly urged that on my way out, I check out the East Village in New York City and find someone named Ann Marie Bresnehan. When he couldn't find her address, he laughed and said, "I guess if you are meant to meet, she'll have to find you."

The next morning, I walked the mile or so from our house on Main Street to Route 495 and began hitchhiking for the first time. By that evening, after several rides, I was in New York City. I asked the first person I met if I was in the East Village.

He responded, "No you're in the Bronx," but I'll take you to the Village." He dropped me off at the intersection of Second Avenue and East Sixth Street in front of the Fillmore East.

Bill Graham[27] opened the Fillmore East on March 8, 1968 in what had been a Yiddish Theater on Second Avenue in what was known as the Yiddish Theater District. The Fillmore East quickly became known as "The Church of Rock and Roll." This is the venue that launched the careers of The Who, Pink Floyd, the Jimi Hendrix Experience, Cream, and Led Zeppelin.

---

[27] Do not confuse Bill Graham the greatest rock promoter of our times with Billy Graham the greatest evangelist of our times

The night I was dropped off at the Fillmore East, someone in the long line waiting to get in, told me that it was closing. The Allman Brothers Band, The J. Geils Band, and Albert King were playing in the final show. I had always dreamt of going to the Fillmore East, hearing the pride of Boston, J Geils, close the Fillmore. It would've been mind-blowing. Unfortunately, the show had been sold out for months.

Because I had no chance of getting in, I went across the street for a Coke at a drugstore that had a lunch counter. As I sat there, I watched the line of people waiting to get into the Fillmore and wondered if Ann Marie would be there. The person on the stool next to me asked if I was going to the show.

"No," I said, "I'm just thinking about the J. Geils Band and wondering if someone named Ann Marie Bresnehan is in that line."

She laughed, "I can tell you she's not. I'm Ann Marie."

I had met many people who identified themselves as peacemakers, but Ann Marie was different. She was more committed to peace and love as essential in our world than anyone I had ever met. She no longer used drugs and was committed to being there 24/7 for any runaway, drug user, or *lost* persons whom she happened to meet. Being there for me meant offering a place to spend the night.

"Any friend of Tony Saulnier can stay as long as he wants."

Ann Marie introduced me to a West Village coffeehouse where, on a memorable night, we saw Telly Savalas (Kojak) play at the Café Feenjon.[28] Neil Young[29], who performed a solo set, was sitting in the audience.

---

[28] A Mecca for lovers of Israeli, Greek, Arabic, Turkish, and Armenian song and dance.

[29] Neil Young was one of the most influential idiosyncratic singer/songwriter of his generation.

Ann Marie also introduced me to Ratner's cheesecake[30] and barley mushroom soup. One night, she introduced me to someone who said that Hollywood had made a film about his life, starring Pat Boone. In David Wilkerson's own words, he tells his story that was the basis for the book and film *Cross and the Switchblade*.

*Ten years ago, I sat in my study reading Life magazine. I casually turned a page, and at first glance, there seemed nothing to interest me. The page showed a pen drawing of a trial taking place in New York City, 350 miles away from home in rural Pennsylvania. I'd never been to New York, and I'd never wanted to go, except perhaps to see the Statue of Liberty.*

*I started to flip the page over, but as I did, something caught my attention. It was the eyes of a figure in the drawing – a boy. He was one of seven boys on trial for murder. I held the magazine closer to get a better look. The artist had captured the look of bewilderment, hatred, and despair in the young boy's features. Suddenly, I began to cry. I wondered, what's the matter with me, impatiently brushing away a tear. Then I looked at the picture more carefully. The boys were all teenagers.*

*They were members of a gang called the Dragons. Beneath the picture was the story of how they had been in Highbridge Park in New York City, when they brutally attacked and killed a fifteen-year-old polio victim named Michael Farmer.*

*The story revolted me. It literally turned my stomach. In our little mountain town, such things seemed mercifully unbelievable. Yet I was dumbfounded by the next thought that sprang into my head, as if it came to me as from outer space. Go to New York and help those boys.*

*The thought startled me. "I'd be a fool to do that," I reasoned. "I know nothing about handling out-of-control kids. And I didn't want to know anything."*

---

[30] Ratner's was a famous Jewish kosher restaurant on the Lower East Side of NYC noted for their cheesecakes.

*It was no use. The idea wouldn't go away. I was compelled to go to New York. And I was to do it at once, while the trial was still in progress.*[31]

David Wilkerson told me that when he got to the courthouse, he asked the judge for permission to talk to the gang members, but the judge rejected his request. As he left, a newspaper photographer took a photo of him carrying a Bible in his hand. The next day, the newspaper headline was "Bible Preacher Interrupts Gang Trial."

David smiled at me and said that although this was one of the most embarrassing moments of his life, the photograph ingratiated him to gang members who now saw him as someone who interrupted a trial on their behalf. This embarrassing picture enabled him to begin a street ministry to young drug addicts and gang members that was eventually called Teen Challenge.

He bought me another piece of cheesecake and enthusiastically chatted on about his new outreach. *Goodniks* was his vision for evangelizing middle-class, restless, and bored youths and trying to prevent them from becoming heavily involved with drugs, alcohol, or violence. He called me a goodnik and invited me to leave Ann Marie's apartment and live with him in the city. I declined and decided to resume my search for my father.

I often think about what would have happened had I stayed. Arriving in Chicago, I located my dad's sister Aunt Esther. Thinking about Aunt Esther and Uncle Leo still revitalizes me. The only time we would see them was on Hanukah. They brought my sister and me the wonderful toys that we saw advertised on television.

Uncle Leo had died, but Aunt Esther hugged me and told me I could stay in her apartment even though she was leaving for Florida within an hour. I had been sleeping on a mat on the floor for the past two weeks so the prospect of a bed sounded great. I accepted and fell into a deep sleep.

---

[31] An excerpt from Dave Wilkerson's testimony found at http://www.worldchallenge.org/about_david_wilkerson

I was awakened by knocks on my door. I heard a voice outside, "Freddie. It's your father."

I opened the door to a stranger. Apparently, Aunt Esther had told him I was there.

When I found my voice, I had a question that I always had wanted to ask, "Why did you leave Mom?"

"It was your grandmother. She persecuted me. I couldn't take it any longer, so I left."

I understood what he meant. I had always had my own problems with Bobe.[32] I myself couldn't go home. I couldn't even call home. I asked Dad what I should do. He suggested that as long as I had hitchhiked this far, why not continue on Route 66 and go to California. You might find a new life there. David Shapiro had not contributed any direction to my old life whatsoever, yet his advice to head west turned out to be profoundly significant.

---

[32] Bobe was my pet name for my grandmother.

# CHAPTER 10

*Well if you ever plan to motor west*
*Just take my way that the highway that the best*
*Get your kicks on Route 66*
*Well it winds from Chicago to L.A.*
*More than 2000 miles all the way*[33]

Buzz Murdock: They make a pretty good map for cars, don't they? But what do they make for guys like me who turn left instead of right?

Todd Stiles: We have to know we're lost before we can find ourselves.

Buzz: That sort of map you make up as you go along."[34]

יהוה (YHWH) said to him, "Because I will be with you, you will strike down Midyan as easily as if they were just one man." Gid'on replied, "If indeed you favor me, would you mind giving me a sign that it is really you talking with me?"[35]

The nation's first duel took place on July 21, 1865 in Springfield, Missouri between "Wild Bill" Hickok and Davis K. Tutt. As they

---

[33] Chuck Berry "Route 66"
[34] "Route 66" TV Show 1962
[35] Judges 6:16-7

stood about seventy-five yards apart and facing each other sideways in dueling positions, both fired almost simultaneously. Tutt missed. Wild Will's shot passed through Tutt's chest. Reeling from the wound, Tutt staggered back to the nearest building before collapsing and dying.

It was just about 6:00 p.m., July 21, 1971, and I had been standing at the Springfield, Missouri ramp to Interstate 44 for hours. I not only felt like collapsing, but I felt I would be dead by morning. For the first time in my life I felt completely abandoned not just by my father, but by all of life. I would never experience or accomplish the things that so many take for granted: I would never finish college, get a real job, get married, or even have sex. Most horrible of all, I felt abandoned by God. I screamed at God. This time I wasn't begging Him for a radio, I was begging Him for my life.

*God is my mom worried about me? Is she angry? Does she want to kill me? Wait a minute God, you can't be real. If you were real, life wouldn't be this way. All my life I believed life only made sense if there was a God and now I know that life doesn't make sense—there is no God. God if there's a chance you are real, I need a sign. I need to see a yellow Corvette stop in front of me now. If it does, I'll know you're real.*

The sound of screeching brakes forced me to turn around. There was a yellow Corvette. The driver rolled down the window and asked me where I was going. I began babbling that he was an angel. He told me I was crazy and drove off. I lost my ride but regained my faith.

I walked to the downtown park where the Hickok and Tutt gunfight was being reenacted by local citizens. I sat down on a bench and wished that Zaydah was there. Zaydah was a fan of Westerns, particularly *High Noon*. As I watched Bill Hickok and Davis Tutt face each other sideways in dueling positions, I understood how that moment in history informed how Fred Zinnemann directed Gary Cooper and Ian MacDonald in the best one-on-one gunfight in movie history. After the re-enacted gunfight, I laid on the bench, looked up at the stars, and remembered a story Zaydah used to tell about Abraham.

As an infant, Abraham was abandoned and left in a cave by his parents. They were afraid that Nimrod would kill Abraham since Nimrod's astrologers foretold that a baby had been born who was destined to shine to the entire world. Abraham cried and cried because he was so hungry. God sent the angel Gabriel, who gave him milk to drink. Abraham stayed in the cave, nurtured by Gabriel until he was three years old, and then he decided to leave.

When he went out, the world was dark. He looked up at the skies and saw the twinkling stars and was amazed by so many millions of little lights. He said, "These must be the most powerful forces in the whole universe. These must be the gods."

But then came the dawn and the stars disappeared. "No," said Abraham, "Those little lights can't be gods because they have disappeared. Something outshines them, I won't worship them anymore."

Then the sun rose and shone in all its glory. Abraham said, "This is the most powerful force. This is God. I will worship this." But toward evening, as the sun set, Abraham understood that the sun is also not God. Then, out of the darkness, the moon rose and shone its light, and Abraham thought, "Yes, this time I have found God."

At that moment the angel Gabriel came down and took Abraham to a fountain of pure water. "Immerse and purify yourself." Then Gabriel revealed that "הוהי (YHWH) is the one God who holds power over all of the Heavens and the Earth. God created the entire world." When Abraham heard the words of the angel, he bowed and prayed to הוהי (YHWH).

Abraham finally understood that we really have no option other than to submit to the higher power. He finally understood that our worship of the stars and planets are actually an excuse for worshipping our own selfish appetites.

As I drifted off to sleep, I thought about my own selfish craving for sex, material things, wealth, power, and even honor. For the first time in my life, I was crying about who I had hurt and not who had hurt me. I had not talked to Mom since I had left New York City. I wanted to call her and let her know how much I loved her. I wanted her to know that Dad had abandoned me yet again but maybe, just maybe, God had found me. I fell asleep before I could call and that night dreamt that I was more closely connected to the God of Abraham than the gods of anything else I had ever longed for.

# CHAPTER 11

*The iron hand, it ain't no match for the iron rod*
*The strongest wall will crumble and fall to a mighty God*
*For all those who have eyes and all those who have ears*
*It is only he who can reduce me to tears*
*Don't you cry and don't you die and don't you burn*
*For like a thief in the night*
*He'll replace wrong with right*
*When he returns*[36]

*Does He Care? Does He Care?*
*Does God lift a finger to get me out of there?*
*When I cry at night, does He feel my plight?*
*Does He Care? Does He Care? Does He Care?*[37]

Sunset Strip welcomed me with a lighted billboard that said LIVE AT THE WHISKY – BUDDY MILES. The solitary sign of significance, however, promised free food at the Tony and Sue Alamo Christian Foundation.

In 1960, Bernie Lazar Hoffman abandoned his Jewish upbringing and heritage and changed his name to Tony Alamo. Tony and his wife Susan began preaching on the streets of Hollywood and West Hollywood. Their

---

[36] Bob Dylan: "When He Returns"
[37] Fred Shapiro (Recorded by Traveler) – "Does He Care"

original audiences were drug addicts, alcoholics, criminals, prostitutes, and runaways. They were considered to be the first of the Jesus People Movement. Their street preaching attracted thousands. They became so popular that they transformed a former Hollywood drug den into a church. The ministry grew quickly, and they soon took over a large farm in Saugus, California.[38]

The bus door opened and the driver invited me to a meeting and free meal at their center in Saugus. I was hungry, so I didn't ask what kind of meeting. I just wanted to make sure that the bus would bring me back to Hollywood. I was promised that it would. I remember nothing about the meeting except that it was in a converted barn, it was loud, and people spoke in gibberish.

After the service, dinner was indeed served, but I was told that eating dinner meant missing the bus back to Hollywood and having to spend the night in sleeping bags. The more the church leaders begged me to stay, the more anxious I became over the possibility that if I stayed I'd never be able to leave. I decided that I'd rather be hungry and homeless in Hollywood than stay at the Tony and Sue Alamo Christian Foundation.

The bus dropped me off at the intersection of Hollywood Boulevard and Highland Avenue. I saw a phone booth and decided that I could finally call Mom. Taped to the inside of the booth was a card with the words "Need Help – call the Hollywood Help Line." I thought I needed the Help Line more than my mom.

A woman named Judy answered the phone. She appeared so empathetic that it wasn't long before I told her my life's story. I told her about being beaten up for being a Christ killer, Zaydah, the drugs, Woodstock, Bobe,

---

[38] Tony Alamo is still a controversial figure. Some praise him and his wife Susan for bringing the Gospel to street people of Hollywood and doing well in the community, (e.g. the Alamos built the Canyon High School football stadium in 1968}. Others see Alamo as a cult leader who brainwashed his followers and there are others who see him as a criminal (e.g. he has been jailed on a variety of charges, including income tax evasion, the theft of his late wife's body, and taking underage girls across state lines for sex).

leaving home, meeting Dad, the yellow Corvette, and Tony and Sue Alamo. Then I asked her if she thought God really cared for me? She guaranteed me he did.

I felt connected to Judy and asked if we could meet. She told me that it was strictly against policy to meet callers. Then she suggested that I find a Grind House (a movie theatre that grinds out old movies twenty-four hours a day for a dollar) and sleep there. Meanwhile, she promised that she'd look for housing and try to find me a job. When I got off the phone, I noticed a Grind House right across the street. I ran over and bought a ticket without noticing what was playing.

I walked into the theater just in time to see Satan (Anton LaVey) have sex with Rosemary (Mia Farrow) and create Rosemary's Baby. This was too much. I headed for the exit. When I reached the last row of the theater, a man stood up, blocked my path and asked, "Are you Fred Shapiro?"

Surprise spurted from the dark theater like steam from a released radiator cap. How could anyone in a Hollywood Grind House at 9 p.m. possibly know me? "Who are you?" I asked.

"I'm Jim, and I'm with the Hollywood Help Line. We usually don't do this, but we traced your call to the phone booth and when I got there I saw the theater. We are a part of the Hollywood Presbyterian Church and our church runs a house where you stay for a while and think more about what you and Judy talked about earlier. Judy will call you in the morning."

On our way to the house on Fairfax Street, Jim suggested we get something to eat and hear a singer named Larry Norman. I had hoped that my first Hollywood concert had been someone famous. I had never heard of Larry Norman. However, I did know the band People! for which he had been the lead singer–.

People! was a one-hit-wonder band whose song "I Love You" had reached number one in the Boston area. According to Norman, when all the band members, except he and co-vocalist Gene Mason, embraced Scientology, other band members issued an ultimatum: join Scientology or leave the band. Norman and Mason left.

Soon after Norman embarked on a solo career, he had a spiritual encounter that forced him to rethink his life. In his own words:

*"I walked up and down Hollywood Boulevard, witnessing to businessmen and hippies, and to whomever the Spirit led me. I spent all of my Capitol Records royalties starting a halfway house and buying clothes and food for new converts."*[39]

Jim and I walked three blocks to an upstairs loft of a converted apartment building. He left to go back to monitor the Help Line, promising someone would drive me to Fairfax St. At the Salt Company, there was food, ping pong, and a stage on which a guy with the longest, blondest hair I had ever seen was singing.

I found a seat at an empty table and was immediately joined by folks from a school called the Jesus Christ Light and Power Company and their instructor Hal Lindsey. Lindsey had just co-authored *The Late Great Planet Earth*.

Without asking if I was interested in hearing his theory, Lindsey took out a Bible and began comparing biblical end-time prophecies with current events. This was the second Bible study I had been forced to sit through in less than four hours and I was beginning to feel that Hollywood had way too many "Jesus Freaks" and not enough people like Ann Marie Bresnehan or Judy.

Now and then, I'd pick up pieces of Lindsay's belief in the Rapture of Christians, which is proceeded by seven years of tribulation and finally the Second Coming of Christ where Christ would establish His Kingdom on Earth.

---

[39] Larry Norman: (October 11, 2006) "The Growth of the Christian Music Industry." Cross Rhythms.

In order to shut him up, I told Lindsey that I was Jewish. Big mistake. This got him only more excited. He told me that the pivotal event that started his eschatological time clock was the foundation of modern Israel in 1948. He was convinced that by 1988, the Rapture would occur. As I tried to listen to the music, I realized that Larry Norman believed in the Rapture, too.

> *Life was filled with guns and war,*
> *And everyone got trampled on the floor,*
> *I wish we'd all been ready*
> *Children died, the days grew cold,*
> *A piece of bread could buy a bag of gold,*
> *I wish we'd all been ready,*
> *There's no time to change your mind,*
> *The Son has come and you've been left behind.*[40]

The New York Times called *The Late Great Planet Earth* the number one non-fiction bestseller of the 1970s. In 1979, it was made into a film narrated by Orson Welles. Does the Second Coming of Christ have the potential to happen in our lifetime? I don't know. What I did know on that hot day on July 9, 1971, I needed a major touch from God if I were to go on living. I needed my sins forgiven if I were not to be left behind. It didn't matter that I was Jewish and had been beaten up by Christians for being Jewish.

I prayed, "Jesus, forgive my sins. Live in my heart."

---

[40] Larry Norman: "I Wish We'd All Been Ready"

# CHAPTER 12

*Picked up a hitchhiker the other day,*
*He said he wasn't going far.*
*He looked so strange I couldn't help myself,*
*I asked, "Please, tell me who you are.*
*He said, hold on its coming. Hold on its coming.*
*He said, hold on it's very near. Hold on it's near.*
*He said, hold on its coming. Hold on its coming.*
*He said, hold on it's almost here. Hold on it's almost here*[41]

I'm not sure how long it took for the reality of my actions to sink in. I do know that I called Anne Marie Bresnehan, telling her that I had just met Jesus and that she ought to consider doing the same thing herself.

She said, "Didn't you know that we were trying to lead you to Jesus in New York? As soon as you left, David Wilkerson prayed that you would somehow come to know Jesus."

For the next few weeks, during the day I'd hitchhike along Santa Monica Boulevard and tell everyone who'd pick me up about Jesus. At night I'd go to Hollywood Boulevard and tell everyone I met about Jesus. One guy, who didn't respond well to my invitation to accept Jesus as Savior, was Peter Wolf, the lead singer from the J. Geils Band. I told him about how I had wanted to see him close the Fillmore East, and about Ann

---

[41] Country Joe McDonald "Hold on It's Coming"

*For Your Tomorrows*

Marie and the yellow Corvette. He didn't listen. But I did meet one man who did.

After sharing my story, he said, "So God proved that He was real by sending a yellow Corvette? I wish He'd show Himself to me."

"All you have to do is ask."

His response activated a biblical bomb that challenged my fresh faith in Jesus.

"I need a ride and I don't have money to pay for it. If God is real, I want you to ask him to make the next car stop and offer me a ride. If He does, I'll give my life to Him."

It was the end of July, but I trembled like a turkey in November. How could God answer a prayer like that? But hadn't I asked God to prove Himself just three weeks ago? What choice did I have? "God, please make the next car stop for him!" Before I could say Amen, he said, "I told you God wasn't real!"

I turned around and saw a taxi heading toward us. This would not be a free ride. The bomb was about to blow up in my face. The cab pulled over and stopped. My friend told the driver that he had no money and that he was just hitchhiking. The cab driver said, "I knew that, hop in!" As the cab took off, the hitchhiker looked through the rear window with an expression of astonishment. I simply took my finger and pointed upward.

# CHAPTER 13

*I had a hard run, runnin' from your window*
*I was all night running, running, Lord, I wonder if you care*
*Test me, test me, why don't you arrest me?*
*Throw me in to the jailhouse Lord, until the sun goes down.*[42]

August 6, 1971, is a memorable night in Grateful Dead history. The show at the Hollywood Palladium is often referred to as the last Warlocks (name of the band prior to the Grateful Dead) show.

I was ready to go back to Haverhill and tell Mom and Heather about meeting Dad and my new relationship with Jesus. My plan was to see the Dead and start hitching immediately afterwards. The concert was forty years ago, so the details are fuzzy.

These are things that I do remember:

- I remember being in the front row.
- I remember the Rowan Brothers opened up the show.
- I remember the New Riders played second.
- I remember a simulated Black Mass on stage.
- I remember the Grateful Dead opened up the show with Bertha.
- I remember hearing the long extended chorus of the song, "Bertha, don't you come around here anymore, anymore,

---

[42] Lyrics by Robert Hunter – Bertha

anymore, anymore," and thinking that Jerry Garcia was singing to me. As I considered leaving, I contemplated how I could make my way through the depths of "dead heads." Suddenly, the crowd parted for me like the Red Sea parted for Moses.

I finally made my way outside the Hollywood Palladium. I was geared up to begin my journey back East when I was waylaid by two elders from the Hollywood Process Church of the Final Judgment. One of the Elders wore the Process symbol of the serpent wrapped around a cross as his belt buckle. I felt as if the engraved snake was about to curl around my waist. The other Elder quickly reached over and with a knife cut the cross that I was wearing off my neck and warned, "You shouldn't have come here tonight."

I felt like the universe was about to end for me. Jesus had offered me a chance at salvation and eternal life but I had gambled it away to see the Warlocks' last show.

Suddenly I discovered what felt like courage. If I was about to take my last breath and be damned for eternity, I didn't want to be judged for just standing there like a piece of meat ready to be thrown to the wolves. If I was going to leave this world, it would be running and not standing. I ran out into the middle of a line of cars on Sunset Boulevard. A cab screeched to a stop in front of me and I got in.

"Are you trying to get killed?" the driver asked.

"No, but I think those two guys in robes are trying to kill me!" To my amazement, he didn't question that and just asked where I was going. It was after midnight, so I decided to spend one more night on Fairfax Street and head home to Haverhill in the morning. When we got to 1542 Fairfax Street, the driver asked, "What does this ride normally cost you?" I confessed that I hadn't taken a Hollywood cab before and pondered why he had asked. He told me that the ride would normally cost about $8.00, but the meter was stuck at $1.80. I went into my pocket and awkwardly offered him the last $2.00 I had. He shrugged and said, "You've had a hard night. Somebody up there must really like you!"

If there's any episode from my life that I'm nervous about sharing, it is this one. Most of my stories don't sound anywhere near as outlandish. This incident didn't stop me from going to Grateful Dead shows. I saw the Grateful Dead a few times after that and enjoyed the shows. I even occasionally play the Dead and Jerry Garcia Band on my Willimantic Gospel radio show.

So why do I share this strange story? It's because of the cab ride. Something happened that night outside the Hollywood Palladium. What did I need deliverance from? I'm not sure. All I know for sure is that I did not cut a cross off of my own neck and that under normal circumstances I would not have had enough money to get to Fairfax Street. I also know that this wasn't about being saved from the Grateful Dead or the Process Church. Maybe God needed to show me that He could stop cab meters. Maybe God needed to show me that $2.00 goes four times as far in his hands. On August 6, 1971, maybe God saved me from myself? Soon I was on Route 66 again. This time I was heading in the opposite direction.

# CHAPTER 14

While hitchhiking home, I became lost and impossibly ended up in Chattanooga. While wandering around the downtown streets, a street preacher came up to me and asked if I was a Christian. I told him that I was.

He then asked, "If I were to rob a bank and was shot before I could confess the crime, would I go to Heaven or Hell?"

I told him, "I wouldn't rob a bank, I'm a Christian."

He then asked me, "Imagine that if somehow I had a moral lapse and then robbed the bank?"

I argued again but eventually realized he wanted an answer so I said, "Because Jesus has forgiven all my sins, I guess I would go to Heaven!"

He was satisfied with my answer and let me leave.

It wasn't long before another preacher approached me (they seemed to be everywhere). He wanted to know if I was a Christian. When I responded that I was, he asked the same question, "If you were to rob a bank and was shot before you could confess the crime, would you go to Heaven or Hell?"

I told him I just answered that question for another preacher and I would go to Heaven.

He looked at me and said, "No you wouldn't, you'd go to hell. He's a Baptist. I'm a Nazarene." I had never heard of Nazarenes before that day but knew I didn't want to be one.

# CHAPTER 15

*Well, it might be in the church house*
*Or it might be on the street*
*Somehow or another every soul has got to meet*
*Well, it might be in the city or it might be in the town*
*One way or another, you're gonna find the higher ground*
*Well, you might be deaf or you might be blind*
*Should put the message right in your mind*
*Might look like a plan or a coalition*
*Or it might be God trying to get your attention*[43]

*The man that is satisfied with the world is without God.*
*The man that has God doesn't need the world.*[44]

When I arrived in Haverhill after meeting Dad and meeting Jesus, I felt like I had fallen into a hell-hole. My mom and sister were supportive of my new-found faith, but other relatives and friends felt I had been brainwashed and worked hard to deprogram me. I was thankful that no one ever told Bobe about my meeting my earthly or Heavenly Father. She lived another fifteen years without knowing that her grandson was meshummad.[45] I hit rock-bottom when a cousin called to ask "how it

---

[43] Keb Mo – "God Trying to Get Your Attention"
[44] Uncle Buddy Robinson- Church of the Nazarene evangelist
[45] In Orthodox Judaism, when one rejects the tenants of Judaism and converts to another religion, they are labeled meshumad ("destroyed one"). In some

felt being a Nazi?" While I shoveled dirt on my grave, I saw Sharon. She wasn't mourning, she was ecstatic.

My friends and I had nicknamed Sharon "groovy girl." Her long, red hair and long legs had always been inviting enough, but during the *Summer of Love* in 1967, her amazing body made it to San Francisco where she lured scores of guys into opposing the Vietnam War and experimented with sex and drugs.

One of the guys who was inveigled into her world was my former Boy Scout troop leader Scott. He would bring her to the rock concerts that my friend was promoting in the very same building where Zaydah and I attended synagogue.[46]

While I was giving my life to Jesus in Hollywood, Sharon was giving her new life to Jesus in Haverhill. She ran over, hugged me, and said, "Praise God," and invited me to the Pilgrim Holiness Church.[47]

---

cases, a funeral is held.

[46] three months ago I preached in that building- it is now a Pentecostal church

[47] Pilgrim Holiness Church is a religious denomination associated with the holiness movement that split from the Methodist Church in 1897. The key beliefs of the holiness movement are (1) regeneration by grace through faith, with the assurance of salvation by the witness of the Holy Spirit; (2) entire sanctification as a second definite work of grace, received by faith, through grace, and accomplished by the baptism and power of the Holy Spirit, by which one is enabled to live a holy life. Holiness groups condemn many actions that our society approves for (e.g., consumption of alcohol, gambling, dancing, movie-going and even men and women swimming together. Other churches that make up the Holiness movement include: Brunstad Christian Church, Christian and Missionary Alliance, Christ's Sanctified Holy Church, Church of Christ (Holiness) U.S.A., Church of Daniel's Band, Church of God (Anderson, Indiana), Church of the Nazarene, Congregational Methodist Church, Bible Missionary Church, Churches of Christ in Christian Union, Evangelical Methodist Church, Free Methodist Church, International Pentecostal Holiness Church, The Salvation Army, Wesleyan Church, Wesleyan Methodist Church (Allegheny Conference), World Gospel Mission, Wesleyan

The church was four blocks from my home, so I went there the next day. I saw Sharon sitting in the front row, but I almost didn't recognize her. Her beautiful, long hair was tied in a bun. Her gorgeous legs were hidden by a long dress that looked like it had been borrowed from Bobe. Her eye-turning looks had become stomach-turning.

With the exception of Sharon, everyone looked to be over seventy years old. I shut my eyes and my mind migrated back to the passionate faith in Zaydah's synagogue. Suddenly I heard a loud thud and felt the energy of a meteor hitting the earth. I opened my eyes and saw that every person had fallen to the floor. Some were wailing, some were rolling, some were pounding their fists, and all were pleading for loved ones who were on their way to hell. I darted out the door.

As I ran down Main Street, a woman who ran even faster caught me and said, "Sometime things can get a little frightening, but think of it as God trying to get your attention! God is impressing on my heart that you must contact Merle Gray, the director of the Nazarene Indian School in Albuquerque. I'm not sure why, I just know you're supposed to do it."

I thought back to the Nazarene street preacher who had proudly distinguished himself from a Baptist, so I politely excused myself. When I arrived home, my mom asked what my plans were and I found myself blurting, "I'm going to Albuquerque."

I called Merle Gray who said, "If you have the faith to come down here, you can go to Bible school here. Classes start next week and the cost of tuition and room and board is $25.00 a month."

I called a Presbyterian minister and asked him about the Nazarenes. He said, "The good thing about the Nazarenes is that they emphasize holiness and devotion to God. The bad news is, if you sin without confessing, you'll lose your salvation."

---

Holiness Alliance (Bartlesville, Oklahoma) and the Original Church of God or Sanctified Church

Living with Nazarenes worried me; I wasn't sure I wanted to be associated with them. On the other hand, $25.00 a month for school, and room and board was a deal I just could not afford to say no to. The next day I was on a Greyhound bus to Albuquerque.

# CHAPTER 16

*I've had Many Tears and Sorrows,
I've had Questions for Tomorrow,
There's Been Times I Didn't Know Right From Wrong.
But In Every Situation, God gave Me Blessed Consolation,
That my trials come just to make me strong* [48]

While at the Nazarene Indian School, I began attending the Southside Church of the Nazarene. Before long, the pastor asked me to lead hymns on Sunday morning. This evolved into my starting a music ministry for teens. When I mentioned to the pastor that I had some experience in promoting concerts, he came up with the idea of bringing Johnny Cash to Albuquerque. I called the House of Cash. Johnny wasn't interested, but many top Gospel artists in the country were. I planned a four-day festival that would be closed by Andrae Crouch.[49]

Although I had absolutely no financial expertise, I was now the producer of what local television and radio personalities were calling a Christian Woodstock. To pay the deposits for the bands, I borrowed money from

---

[48] Andrae Crouch: "Through it All"
[49] Crouch was a key figure in the Jesus Music movement of the 1960s and 1970s and was and helped bridge the gap between black and white Christian music. His songs have been recorded by several secular artists (e.g. Elvis Presley, Paul Simon) and in 1996, a tribute CD of his music won a Grammy Award.

one of the teachers at the school and agreed to pay him back from ticket sales. Due to slapdash bookkeeping and implausibly low ticket prices, on the opening night of the festival, I was $12,000 in the hole. The one especially horrific experience on opening night still haunts me.

The opening act of the festival was a popular Southern Gospel family band to whom I still owed $200 of a $1,000 honorarium. When the paterfamilias came up to me and requested to talk to me on their bus, I sensed a sea of trouble. As he shook my hand, I felt millions of fleas biting into every inch of my arm. His eyes bored into my soul; my chest felt invaded. He clenched his fist and warned, "I heard that you may not have enough money to pay all the bands. I just wanted you to know that if you were thinking of shorting anyone, it had better not be us. You know I haven't always been a Christian. As soon as our set ends I want the other $200 that you owe us." Somehow the custodian of the Albuquerque Convention Center was in earshot of the conversation and shook his head incredulously.

From the back of the auditorium, the custodian watched the Southern Gospel family take the stage and, miraculously, the persecutor who had promised me peril was transformed into preacher. His clenched fist was now part of a hand that was being lifted toward God as he promised "We're not about singing, we're about praising the Lord." Forty-five minutes later, he ended their set by inviting people to come forward to pray and accept Jesus. With tears in his eyes, he promised that he would momentarily come down and pray with each person, but he needed to so something important first. The custodian looked at me and said, "You do know what that something is, right?"

Fortunately, during their set, we had sold enough tickets to pay him the $200. This awful memory was overcome by the generosity of almost everyone else. I was especially inspired by Andrae Crouch, the kindest and most merciful person I've ever met, who agreed to waive his $2,500 fee.

Then there was Abe, an Orthodox Jewish deli owner who was selling sandwiches at the convention center. When he heard that I did not have enough money to pay the rental fee of the convention center, he took me aside and whispered, "I'll be your Messiah and pay for the convention center, but I won't pay for *goyische* music about Jesus."[50]

Finally there was Ron Salisbury, who not only performed but also helped me negotiate settlements with the other bands. Today Ron is the pastor of New Life Community Church in Pismo Beach, CA.

By the end of the week, I saw the Logos Festival as a total embarrassment. I felt like I had been standing unprepared in the face of a hurricane. I couldn't face anyone and once again, I was ready to run, but I didn't know where to run to.

The following Sunday, a traveling team from Pasadena Nazarene College came to the Southside Church of the Nazarene. They closed the service with Andrae Crouch's "I'm Coming Home."

> *I drifted so far away from the lord now I'm coming home.*
> *I'm so tired of sin can't find peace within. I'm coming home.*

As they sang, I wept, came forward to ask forgiveness, and made a new commitment to Jesus. The person who prayed with me was a sophomore named Rick Fauss. After I shared my testimony with him, he let me know that Pasadena College was about to move to a beautiful campus in a seaside community in San Diego. Some have called Point Loma Nazarene University the most beautiful campus in the world.

I confessed that I had been kicked out of a junior college. He looked at me and said, "Are you telling me that God won't finish what he started in your life? God is going to grow you and prepare you for leadership somewhere, why not in San Diego?"

I told him that I could barely afford my $25 a month at the Nazarene school. He said that if God wanted me at Point Loma College, finances wouldn't be a problem. The next day I called Dr. James Jackson, the

---

[50] Goyische is a Yiddish term for someone/thing which is not Jewish..

Dean of Pasadena College, and shared my testimony, educational background, and finances. He echoed the same offer Merle Gray had made to me: "If you have faith enough to come down here, we will find a place for you. Classes start next week."

# CHAPTER 17

*Sheriff Bart:*    *I'm rapidly becoming a big Underground success in this town.*

*Gunslinger Jim:*    *See? In another twenty-five years, you'll be able to shake their hands in broad daylight.*[51]

A week later, a 23-year-old, fat, lisping, lox- and bagel-loving Yankee who believed in Jesus was living with a group of nineteen to twenty-one- year-old Nazarene surfers. Most classmates knew each other from church, camp meeting week, and the Nazarene Young People's Society (NYPS). I was an outcast. Nevertheless, God spoke to me in a dream about being class president.

There were two other classmates running, Rob and Julie, both past NYPS presidents. How could I have thought that it was possible for me not to look like a fool running against them? The night before the election, I sat on a hill overlooking the freshman and sophomore welcome activities. Outside of my roommate, I had met no other freshmen. I noticed Rob and Julie shaking hands, giving hugs, and laughing with their support groups. I hadn't noticed Gumby approaching until he sat down beside me.

---

[51] "Blazing Saddles" screenplay by Mel Brooks, Norman Steinberg, Andrew Bergman, Richard Pryor, Alan Uger

"My name's David. People call me Gumby and I'm from Los Angeles. Who are you?"

"I'm Fred Shapiro from Boston."

"Hey Boston, how come you're not at the Eastern Nazarene College, in Quincy? Wait a minute, Fred Shapiro, are you the Fred that is running for freshmen class president?"

"Yeah I am, but I think it was a big mistake. I don't know anybody here. It was a stupid idea! There is no way I will get any votes."

"Don't think that way, Boston, I think you'd be a great president. I'm going to get you elected!"

I laughed at the idea that a Woody Allen look-alike, nicknamed Gumby, could get me elected. I still knew I had no chance but Gumby made me laugh and treated me kindly. I felt good for the first time since I'd arrived in San Diego.

Election Day was also the first day of classes. I had little time to be depressed with the prospect of starting a new educational chapter in my life beginning ahead of me. Gumby and Rick were even in two of my religion classes.

That day, every time I passed the polling center, I saw Gumby laughing and chatting with everyone. At dinner, Gumby came over to my table and suggested that we go to a movie and take my mind off the ballot counting. The movie was *Blazing Saddles*. I hadn't been to a movie in a long time and my laughter made me wonder what I was doing in a conservative Christian college.[52] But there were twenty other Nazarene students there and they were laughing just as hard as I was, so I assumed we'd all be forgiven.

---

[52] In 1973, the Nazarene Church did not support attending films.

When we returned to the dorm, there was an invitation taped to my door that said to meet with members of a fraternity. Gumby said, "That can only mean one thing! You won the election!"

Once again, God had moved miraculously in order to change my life and the community I was living in. Next year, I was voted Director of Student Activities. My success in that position opened the door for me to preach in Nazarene churches in California and Arizona.

I wanted to use this preaching tour as a test of God's faithfulness. Would God take care of me if I started out with no money and simply the clothes on my back? Three miracle stories from that preaching tour still impact me.

# CHAPTER 18

*Did ya find a directing sign?*
*On the straight and narrow highway?*
*Would you mind a reflecting sign?*
*Just let it shine, within your mind*
*And show you the colors that are real*[53]

Blood Sweat and Tear's "Spinning Wheel" is about a spinning wheel and it's about pride. Did David Clayton-Thomas know about the greatest spinner of all?

Arachne, a Greek goddess, was such an amazing spinner (or weaver) that people came from all around to see her beautiful cloth. She bragged that she was a better spinner than the goddess Athena. This angered Athena so much she challenged Arachne to a weaving contest.

Athena's weaving pattern depicted the gods and goddesses sitting together on Mt. Olympus doing good deeds for people. Arachne's weaving pattern showed gods and goddesses getting drunk and making a mess of things. Arachne's weaving was clearly superior to Athena's, but Athena was so angered by Arachne's smugness and egotistical attitude that the goddess pointed her magical finger at Arachne. Arachne's nose and ears shrank, her hair fell out, her arms and legs got long and skinny. Arachne shrank until she was just a little spider.

---

[53] David Clayton Thomas – "Spinnin' Wheel" sung by Blood Sweat and Tears

"You want to spin," cried Athena, "go ahead and spin!"

I share the myth because my success at Point Loma was making it difficult for me to remember my place. In hindsight, I felt smugger, more self-important than everybody around me, perhaps even God. Sometimes I think I still do.

I was preaching at a Nazarene church in Ventura, California on a Wednesday night. After the service, the pastor drove me to the train station and asked if I'd like him to phone the pastor in San Jose and tell him that I'd be arriving a few days early. I told him I'd take care of it and would be at the church on Saturday. He asked if I was sure. I said I was. As soon as he left, I regretted my rash decision.

While on the train, I hoped and prayed that the pastor would call the church. When I got to San Jose, there was no sign saying "Welcome Fred Shapiro." I was alone in the tenth largest city in the USA. Furthermore, I had less than $30 in my pocket to last me for three days.

My desire to do my own thing had become more important than my original vision of discovering God's faithfulness and His provision. Would God ever heal me of my pride?

I found the cheapest hotel I could find at $7 a night. That left me with $3 a day for food. It seemed feasible until I got up to the room.

I could hear the hookers turning tricks in the next room. The smell of pot mixed with the smell of vomit, urine, and bodily fluids in the hallway. These wretched conditions forced me to cry out to God, confessing my sin, and hoping that the sounds, the stink, and the sin would cease. It just got worse. However, God was silent that night.

I had to get away from that degradation, so I left my room and walked two or three miles until I saw an all-night theater similar to the one I had found on Hollywood Boulevard. This time I checked the marquee to see what was playing. It was Clint Eastwood and George Kennedy in *The Eiger Sanction*. Although it was another $3.00 that I could hardly afford, it looked more comfortable than the hotel. Between praying and sleeping, I never really watched the film. I will have to watch it someday, just to see what I missed.

I left the theater and noticed a sandwich shop next door. Before I could enter, a voice called out "Fred Shapiro!" It was Jamie Fauss, Rick Fauss' cousin who lived in Modesto, which was about eighty-five miles away. No word or combination of words accurately describe what I felt at that moment.

"Jamie, what are you doing in San Jose?"

"I work at the church where you're preaching. The pastor from Ventura called. We went down to the station to meet you, but we were late and you were gone. We've looked all over town and were just getting ready to quit when Luann said, 'We haven't prayed yet'. Just as we finished, you turned the corner!"

Jamie and Luann drove me back to the hotel to get my stuff and the manager even refunded the money for the next two nights. I spent the next three days relaxing on a ranch run by college students. God was beginning to deliver me from my pride and arrogance. I was beginning to believe that I didn't have to be stingy with God's grace or my resources.

# CHAPTER 19

Bobcat Goldthwait, who is known for his stand-up comedy and his appearances in the Police Academy movies, is now directing critically acclaimed films. His latest film *Willow Creek* is about Bigfoot.

The premise of Willow Creek is about a group of people heading into the forests of the Pacific Northwest seeking Sasquatch (Bigfoot) and getting more than they bargained for.

I had to hitchhike over 300 miles from San Jose to Willow Creek. I wasn't looking for Sasquatch, I was looking for the Willow Creek Church of the Nazarene where Gumby's brother in law was the pastor. Like Goldthwait's subjects searching for Sasquatch, I, too, got a lot more than I bargained for.

I was about fifty miles south of Willow Creek, when I was dropped off unexpectedly at a service station where I met a man and woman in a broken-down car.

I wish I could remember what had been wrong with the car!

I wish I could remember exactly what it would have cost to fix it!

All I remember is that the couple had no money and that it would cost exactly every penny I had to pay for the repairs. The couple agreed to take me to Willow Creek if I paid for the repairs. I reasoned that I'd be speaking in a church where I was certain to earn a decent pay from my best friend's brother-in-law, so I gave them the money.

In Willow Creek, I told the pastor my story of helping that couple.

He nervously laughed and said, "I sure hope we get a few more people than we usually get."

On Sunday, there were seven members and one visitor attending the service. I was in trouble. There was no way that this offering could be more than $35, and I had no other speaking engagement until I got to Phoenix, Arizona, which was over 1,000 miles away.

I tried to hide my disappointment at the size of the offering. I'm not sure if I did. After the service, everyone left except for the pastor and the visitor.

The visitor walked over to me and asked, "Are you familiar with the Naval Training Center in Point Loma?" The center was about a mile from the Point Loma College, so I told her I knew of it. What I didn't tell her was that while going to school, I was working at the center as a bartender at the Burger and Brew. Remember, Nazarenes don't drink.

She took my hand and said, "My nephew is at the Training Center and is very lonely. Is there any way you can look after him for me?"

I still didn't want to admit where I worked, "I'm not sure I can do that, the Center is off-limits to civilians."

She responded, "He told me about a place called the Burger and Brew and invited me there. I thought if I can get in there you could get in also."

She told me her nephew's name and gave me $200. I never found her nephew so I've always felt a bit guilty about keeping her money. By the time I returned to San Diego, I no longer had the job. Her $200, however, got me to Phoenix, where a comment made at the end of my service prepared me for all that would happen when I returned to Point Loma.

# CHAPTER 20

The service in Phoenix had been powerful, and many had come forward to receive Christ. After the service, a woman walked up to me and said, "The Holy Spirit is all around you. It's so thick I can't even touch you." Then she added, "You need to leave the Nazarene church, it will strangle you."

I asked, "How can you say that? Aren't you a Nazarene?"

She smiled saying, "its okay for me, I was born into it—you weren't. Trust me it will strangle you!"

I had begun my preaching tour by hitchhiking toward Ventura with no money in my pocket. I returned to Point Loma in a rented, brand new Ford LTD. God had taken very good care of me. Furthermore, I was soon hired as the advance person for the Love Song reunion tour.[54]

I couldn't believe it. The most popular Christian rock band in the world had just hired me to book halls and arrange dates for their tour. I was not only Director of Activities; I was working for Love Song. My classes

---

[54] Love Song was one of the first Christian rock bands and was founded in 1970 by Chuck Girard, Tommy Coomes, Jay Truax, and Fred Field. Denny Correll, (Blues Image) also sang with the band at one time. Another latter-day member was Phil Keaggy. In 1976 they did a reunion tour that was captured on their double-live album Feel the Love.

could wait. I knew what I wanted to do with my life: I wanted to work in either an ad agency or public relations firm. Then Moishe Rosen spoke in a chapel service I attended.

Moishe Rosen had just left the American Board of Missions to the Jews in 1970 to establish Jews for Jesus, a ministry that would focus on Evangelism to the Jewish people. Twenty-seven years later, the Conservative Baptist Association named him a "Hero of the Faith."

I had never met another Jew who believed in Jesus and still lived as a Jew. Moishe told me that he had heard me preach in Berkley, California that past summer and then shocked me by repeating the advice of the woman in Phoenix Arizona, "Get out of the Nazarene Church before it strangles you."

I laughed and reminded him that the Nazarene Church had not only changed my life but was opening its doors for him so that he could develop his new vision of Jewish Evangelism. He agreed but also reminded me that doors that open quickly can also slam shut and hurt you.

It wasn't long before that door slammed shut on me. Maybe it was my job at the Burger and Brew. Maybe it was my regular attendance at a local movie theater. Maybe it was a poem that I had written for a local poetry contest. Maybe it was because I had run a red light and smashed into a police cruiser with a school van at 3:00 a.m.

Whatever the reason, I was asked to resign my post as Activity Director. I could have stayed on as a student, but I couldn't live with that. I chose to leave Point Loma College.

I moved into a room in a downtown San Diego hotel and got a job at the Cabrillo Theatre. My job was to take tickets, run the concession stand, wake up drunks, baby-sit hookers' kids, and make sure that no one was arrested. In between shifts, I'd preach in Horton Plaza, the downtown park frequented by San Diego's homeless and destitute.

After about three months, the manager congratulated me; I was promoted to the assistant manager of another theater in the chain. When he told me that we could walk there, my heart sank. There was only one theater in walking distance—a Pussycat Theatre. I had backslid from being the Director of Student Activities at a Nazarene College to the assistant manager of an X-rated theater.

I called Moishe Rosen in San Rafael and told him everything that had happened. There was a long pause and then an "Oy." After another pause, he said he'd wire me money to get on a Greyhound bus and come to San Rafael immediately.

# CHAPTER 21

*When God asked Adam, "Where are you?" It was not because the Almighty Creator had failing sight or suddenly forgot the geography of the Garden of Eden. No, He was asking Adam to take stock and gain perspective regarding his spiritual condition in the face of adversity, be it physical or spiritual. God asks us where we are—not because He doesn't know, but because He wants us to gain perspective, to see if we are where we should be.*[55]

When I arrived in San Rafael, Moishe immediately took me under his wing. I accompanied him on all of his speaking engagements. He insisted that I begin using my Hebrew name Ephraim. Every night from the pulpit, he would introduce me as a messed up young man whom, for some wild reason, Moishe still believed in. Until I could find a place to live, I stayed with a Jews for Jesus missionary family, Irving Kugler and his wife.

After a two-week orientation, Moishe told me that his ultimate goal was to make me a part of The Liberated Wailing Wall, the musical evangelistic team.[56] First, however, he wanted me to learn each job in the ministry.

---

[55] Moishe Rosen: "Adversity Brings Opportunity"

[56] The Liberated Wailing Wall was the Jews for Jesus mobile evangelistic music team for over 30 years. They were retired by Jews for Jesus in 2012 shortly after their 12th albums- Never Forget.

*For Your Tomorrows*

My first job at Jews for Jesus was working in the print shop. My boss was Irving Kugler. I am klutzy, inartistic, and messy. I'm not at all enthusiastic about printing, folding, and cutting the evangelistic literature that Jews for Jesus passed out on the streets and in the airports. The hardest part was that because I lived with Irving, I had to live with the consequences of my mistakes and failures 24/7.

One day, I was eating my lunch at a bus stop while looking at apartment classifieds. Three beautiful women noticed my Jews for Jesus T-shirt and sat down next to me.

The conversation went something like this:

*Girls:* *Wow, you're with Jews for Jesus. Our church loves you guys. We give money to you.*

*Me:* *Cool, what church is that?*

*Girls:* *Church of the Open Door. We meet in the Carpenter's Hall on Lindaro Street every Sunday. You should come.*

*Me:* *I'm usually with Moishe on Sunday. Maybe I could meet you girls some other time.*

*Girls:* *That would be great. We spend a lot of time at our church. By the way, are you looking for an apartment?*

*Me:* *Yeah.*

*Girls:* *I bet if you came to our church, you'd find one.*

*Me:* *That would be cool, and you girls would be there right?*

*Girls:* *We never miss a service. You really should come!*

When I got back to work, I asked other Jews for Jesus missionaries about the church. Some attended the church and gave me a little history. The key pastor was Kent Philpott who in 1967, while attending seminary, felt the calling to connect with the Jesus People Movement.

In 1972, he and Mark Buckley, Bob Hymers, Roger Hoffman, Mike Riley, and Dick Bruner began the Church of the Open Door in Mill Valley. It had recently moved to the Carpenter's Hall in San Rafael. No one at the Church of the Open Door knew anyone who looked like the three women I had met.

I wasn't scheduled to go with Moishe to a church on Sunday, so I decided that I would attend the Church of the Open Door. I did not see any of the three girls there. In fact, over the next year and a half, I became deeply involved in the church and I never saw one of them. I'm convinced God used three angels to bring me to the Open Door, and then God found a way to keep me there.

I had never been to church in a union hall, I was uncomfortable with the sermon and I was uncomfortable with speaking in "tongues."[57] I felt no comfort until a singer/guitarist closed the service by singing a song of commitment. I didn't know the song, but I knew the voice.

After church, I went over to him and said, "You sound just like the lead singer of Orpheus." He said, "You're right, I was the lead singer of Orpheus. I'm Bruce Arnold."

I told him I was from Haverhill and that I had interviewed him eight years earlier. He told me that he was from Worcester and that he was

---

[57] Speaking in tongues is the New Testament phenomena where a person speaks in a language that is unknown to him. This language is either the language of angels or other earthly languages (1 Cor. 13:1). It occurred in Acts 2 at Pentecost and also in the Corinthian Church as is described in one Corinthians 14. Today there is much debate as to the validity of speaking in tongues, especially since there is so much misuse of it in Christian circles. Some churches argue that spiritual gifts (e.g. speaking in tongues, prophecy, and healing) ceased with the completion of the New Testament (one Cor. 13:8-12). Others maintain that spiritual gifts are still for the church today (1 Cor. 1:7).

now one of the pastors in the Church of the Open Door. He then invited me to live in one of the houses that the Church of the Open Door was renting.

How could I say no to the Orpheus lead singer who had sung "Can't Find the Time"?

As I got more involved with the Church of the Open Door, both Moishe and I sensed that my experiences with Jews for Jesus were designed to position me to walk into the Church of the Open Door. Walking through that door introduced me to some of the sweetest people I've ever met in my life: Reverend Jim and Beverly Smith, Michael and Buffy Petit, Kathy Their, Pam Troyer and Reverend Kent Philpott.

One of the most extraordinary moments in my life was when Pastor Kent called and asked if I'd like to manage the Christian General Store in San Francisco and be one of the pastors at the San Francisco Church of the Open Door.

# CHAPTER 22

Doctor: There is one outside chance of a cure. I think of it as shock treatment. As I say, there is an outside chance.

Chris MacNeil: Will you just name it, for God's sake? What is it?

Doctor: Do you have any religious beliefs?

Chris MacNeil: No.

Doctor: What about your daughter?

Chris MacNeil: No, why?

Doctor: Have you ever heard of exorcism? It's a stylized ritual in which rabbis or priests try to drive out the so-called invading spirit. It's pretty much discarded these days, except by the Catholics who keep it in the closet as a sort of embarrassment. It has worked in fact, although not for the reason they think, of course. It was purely the force of suggestion. The victim's belief in possession helped cause it. And just in the same way, this belief in the power of exorcism can make it disappear[58]

---

[58] William Peter Blatty; Screenplay of the Exorcist 1973

*There is no need at all to make long discourses; it's enough to stretch out hands and say: "Lord as you will and as you know, have mercy." He knows very well what we need and He shows us His mercy.*[59]

In 1973, William Friedkin's *The Exorcist* introduced spiritual warfare into American culture.[60] Adapted from the 1971 novel by William Peter Blatty (who also wrote the screenplay), *The Exorcist* is based on the 1949 exorcism case of Roland Doe. The film was nominated for ten Academy Awards and was the first horror film ever to be nominated for Best Picture. Entertainment Weekly named it the scariest film of all time and the Library of Congress selected the film to be preserved as part of its National Film Registry. As a result of *The Exorcist*, churches began to take exorcism seriously.

Although my two co-pastors, Bob and Dennis, and all the other pastors in the Church of the Open Door took spiritual warfare seriously, my experiences in the Process Church had persuaded me that the idea of a literal devil was silly. I was the pastor chosen to manage our bookstore. I was also the pastor that led our Monday night Bible study.

One Monday night, a young woman named Tara came to our study and asked for prayer. She claimed that she was getting bad headaches and they were especially excruciating whenever she wanted to pray. It was our church's custom to have women in the church lay hands on and pray for women and that men do the same for men. As hands were laid on Tara, she began to shake. I wasn't needed during the prayer for her, so I went into another room and softly prayed, "God I've never believed in demons but if demons are behind this, please let me know."

In answer to that prayer, instantly I heard Tara scream. As I looked up, she broke free from the prayer circle and ran toward me and knelt at my feet.

---

[59] 4th century Egyptian monk Macarius

[60] Spiritual warfare is the term that many Christians use to refer to methods of taking a stand against supernatural evil forces. Among Christians, the most common form of spiritual warfare is prayer. Other practices may include exorcisms, laying-on of hands, fasting, or anointing with oil.

My second prayer of deliverance was something like, *Jesus, I can't handle this s\*\*\*, but you can. Please take care of Tara!*

Immediately Tara began to pray and thank God. Her headaches were gone. Tara would eventually become a member of the San Francisco Church of the Open Door. I've asked myself many times whether Tara was acting or pretending. I really didn't know.

I keep going back to the idea that there is absolutely no way she could've heard my first prayer from the other room. I was now convinced that the God who shows me yellow Corvettes, finds me in Grind Houses, finds my transistor radio, directs me to a shelter in the East Village, and sends me angels, can take away headaches. Three days later, God would use another miracle to convince me further of the reality of spiritual warfare.

Chas was a stranger who walked into our bookstore to buy a Bible. When he touched the Bible he began getting a headache and getting dizzy. I wondered why a person would begin to get a headache as she touched a Bible and then I remembered Tara. I asked him if he'd like me to pray for him. Before he could answer, I authoritatively said, "In the name of Jesus, Satan set this man free. Your authority is over!"

Chas' headache immediately went away. He wanted to know more about me and the church I co-pastored. I invited him home with me for dinner and he accepted. Chas became a member of our church and eventually so did his brother. Tara and Chas helped me believe in Jesus as a deliverer. I only wish Satan's authority had been broken in my life.

I was about to enter into a season of my life where moments of healing would not be evident. Not long after being with Tara and Chas, I was fired from my job as bookstore manager and pastor. I had kept poor records and thoughtlessly ordered too much merchandise on credit.

I could have stayed in the house on Thirty-Seventh Avenue, but I couldn't live with the disgrace. I ran from the Church of the Open Door the same way I had run from Point Loma College a year earlier—by renting a room in a downtown fleabag hotel. It was a year before I'd experience another miracle.

# CHAPTER 23

*It's an odd thing, but anyone who disappears is said to be seen in San Francisco. It must be a delightful city and possess all the attractions of the next world.*[61]

When I left the Church of the Open Door, I became a Fuller Brush salesman. I made most of my sales by going into downtown piano bars and singing songs like "If I Were a Rich Man" and changing lyrics to promote products. One night while singing in Joe Nobriga's Showcase, I got the attention of Bobby McFerrin's pianist, Dick Turner.

"You've got a really good voice but why are you singing crap?"

I replied, "I'm trying to sell these brushes and singing beats knocking on doors."

Dick Turner committed himself to helping me learn new music and develop a vocal style. Because of Dick's influence, I began gaining an appreciation for swing and jazz vocalists such as Ella Fitzgerald, Mel Torme, Anita O'Day, and Eddie Jefferson. I began memorizing their scat lines.

Jazz was beginning to replace Jesus as my passion. I no longer spent my Sundays in church. I spent my Sunday mornings learning songs and

---

[61] Oscar Wilde

Sunday afternoons trying them out in jazz clubs, like Pier 23. Because people like Bobby McFerrin, Mark Murphy, and Tuck and Patty were singing in San Francisco, it was, of course, impossible for me to make a living singing jazz. I changed my venue. I began attending jam sessions at rock and blues clubs on Sunday nights, and it wasn't long before I put a rock band together.

My first gig in San Francisco was at the Golden Horse Saloon located on Mason Street between Eddy and Ellis Street. Eddy Ellis would become my stage name. Fred Shapiro was dead. Then one night, Jesus showed up at an Eddy Ellis show.

During the first set, our guitarist noticed a man dressed in a suit in the audience. Was he an agent? A reporter? A lawyer? A month earlier, one of Senator Ted Kennedy's aides had approached me about working on his presidential campaign. Was this a follow-up visit? During the break, I went over to him. He introduced himself as Gary Wilkerson, son of Dave Wilkerson who was in town for a crusade.[62]

The Wilkerson's had heard about a San Francisco singer who now and then talked a lot about Jesus during the show.

"Eddy Ellis, you sound to me like a backslidden Christian."

"Why do you say I am backslidden?"

"You can't sing in those places and still be following Christ", he replied.

Then Gary Wilkerson made me an offer that would change my life. "I want you to figure out all of your debts, everything you owe to anybody. If you agree to come back to Texas with my dad and me, we will pay off all of your debts. I'll give you a couple of days to think about it."

I told him about meeting his Dad at Ann Marie Bresnehan's and also told him about the yellow Corvette, Point Loma College, and Church of the Open Door.

---

[62] The same Dave Wilkerson that I met 11 years earlier in the East Village

Gary sighed and said, "Is God finally getting your attention? Look at all the signs he has given you."

Three days later was the Jonestown, Guyana massacre.[63] A week after the massacre, Mayor Moscone and Harvey Milk were shot[64]. Those were the signs I needed. I left San Francisco and took my heart with me on November 29th—my birthday.

---

[63] "Jonestown" was the informal name for the Peoples Temple Agricultural Project in Guyana, a community formed by members of the San Francisco Peoples Temple pastored by Reverend Jim Jones. On November 18, 1978, 918 of his Jones's followers died in a mass suicide. At Jones's command, five others were shot by Temple member at a nearby Port Kaituma airstrip. The victims included United States Congressman Leo Ryan.

[64] On November 27, 1978, San Francisco Mayor George Moscone and San Francisco Supervisor Harvey Milk were shot and killed in City Hall by former Supervisor Dan White. White was subsequently convicted of voluntary manslaughter and served just over 5 years in prison. This verdict and light sentence sparked the "White Night riots." White ultimately committed suicide in 1985, a little more than a year after his release from prison.

# CHAPTER 24

*We live that our souls may grow. The development of the soul is the purpose of existence. God Almighty is trying to obtain some decent association for Himself.*[65]

After spending some time with the Wilkerson's in Lindale, Texas, I was told that my new home would be the Teen Challenge center in Hungerford, Texas. On the day before I came to Teen Challenge, Gary Wilkerson took me out to dinner and a movie.

At dinner he said, "This will be the last movie that you see for quite a while so I'll let you choose."

I chose *The Hunter* with Steve McQueen. Ironically, this was the last film Steve McQueen ever made.

As we said our goodbyes, Gary said, "You need to know that the particular Teen Challenge we're sending you to is a highly militant program. It is a lot like boot camp and less than 15 percent who start, finish. On the positive side, at Teen Challenge, you will discover the things about yourself that keep tripping you up and are keeping you from living a truly purposeful life for Christ. I promise that you will experience the miraculous hand of God in ways that you can't even imagine." Then he added, "One more promise and this has to remain just

---

[65] John G. Lake

between us. Once you graduate from Teen Challenge, David Wilkerson Ministries will give you a scholarship to the college of your choice. When things get hard and they will, just remember what I am promising you right now."

I arrived at Houston Airport where one of the staff of Teen Challenge met me and drove me the fifty-four miles to Hungerford, Texas. When I arrived, I met the director, Dave Kirschke.

Dave Kirschke had been planning to be a missionary in Senegal, West Africa. But that didn't happen. In 1974, while studying for the mission field in the inner city of Houston, he sensed a calling to the destitute and homeless of Houston. He opened up his home to them.

It wasn't long before he and his wife purchased an abandoned high school in Hungerford, Texas. They had only been in Hungerford, Texas for three months when I arrived at the center. The first thing Dave Kirschke told me was that I needed to forget everything about my past, including any previous Christian experiences.

"You enter Teen Challenge with a clean slate. You are a 'Baby Christian' without a voice. As far as you are concerned, staff is God's Word."

Then he asked me to sign a promise before God that if I leave Teen Challenge before completing the yearlong program, I agree to be in rebellion and excommunicated from God's kingdom. The only way to receive forgiveness from God was to start the program over from the beginning.

Gary was correct. At the Teen Challenge, I discovered the roots of my anger and resentment that had short-circuited any purposeful Christ-centered living. Perhaps, more importantly, through the teaching of Dave Kirschke's dad, William Kirschke, I began to develop a biblical basis for the miracles that I had taken for granted.

William Kirschke was a protégé of John G. Lake, the early twentieth century minister who was an instrument of healings. He conducted over 100,000 healings between 1915 and 1920.

Lake's friends included Sir Arthur Conan Doyle and Ehrich Weisz (aka Harry Houdini). I was an eyewitness to one of the miracles at Teen Challenge.

One night, Dave Kirschke rang the bell that was a call for us to report to the chapel. Our fishing team had returned with absolutely no fish. The situation was especially dire because our food supply was short. The day before, we had caught an armadillo and cooked the meat in chili.

At the meeting, Dave Kirschke read Luke 5: 4-6:

> *When Jesus finished speaking, He said to Simon, "Put out into the deep water, and let down your nets for a catch." Simon answered, "Master, we have worked all night long but have caught nothing. Yet if you say so, I will let down the nets." When they had done this, they caught so many fish that their nets were beginning to break.*

He then instructed the fishing team to go back to the same place they were before, but only deeper. At about 1:00 a.m., three bells were sounded. This was a call to meet in the cafeteria. There were so many fish that it took seven of us three hours to clean them all.

I was in charge of the kitchen that week, so it was my responsibility to close up when all of the work was done. Just as I was about to turn off the lights, a Texas Ranger appeared at the kitchen door.

"I know it's late, but we saw the lights and hoped it would be all right to come in. Last night we caught some poachers with three deer. Rather than fining them, we had the poachers cut and clean the meat. We will deliver it when they are finished." Our food shortage was solved, not once, but twice.

This incident remains one of the most profound examples of God's movement that I've ever experienced. Sadly, when God moves, Satan counterattacks. That night in the kitchen was the last time I experienced joy at Teen Challenge.

# CHAPTER 25

Sometimes it's hard to tell the difference between what God is doing and what Satan is doing. I had been at Teen Challenge for about eight months when Jay, the assistant director of Teen Challenge, asked, "What would you do if you were slandered in a newspaper or magazine?"

I quickly said, "I'd sue."

He put his head down, "I was afraid you'd say that."

He then showed me the headline of Dave Wilkerson's latest newsletter: *"Homosexual Rock Singer Is Serving Christ and Growing in the Spirit"*

By the end of the day, I was getting calls from people throughout the country for prayer and counseling. Jay joked, "You're finally becoming the celebrity you always wanted to be."

I laughed but was also frustrated. Why would Dave Wilkerson write that I was homosexual?

I never sued Dave Wilkerson, and I wasn't even angry with him, but I was confused about how a man of God whom I respected so much could have been so wrong about who I was. And if he couldn't be trusted, how could I trust the leaders at Teen Challenge with the molding of my spiritual identity?

I began to question the directives that the staff gave me. It all came to a head when a staff member asked, "If I said cut out your tongue, would you do it?"

I jokingly said, "I'd need to see that Word confirmed in scripture."

The staffer didn't laugh and replied, "The Bible is a sword, and swords in the hands of baby Christians are dangerous."

I was then put into isolation until I repented.

I had been in isolation about eight hours and was repeatedly thinking over two questions: First, how could everything I had ever learned about Christ before I got there have a negative bearing on my spiritual identity? Second, and more crucial, if I left the program, was I rebelling against God and damning myself to hell?

At about 10:00 p.m., a staff member came in to tell me I had a phone call. It was Dave Wilkerson. He apologized for the mistake contained in his newsletter and assured me that the misprint had occurred because I had been performing in a gay nightclub. He then encouraged me to stick out the program for the next four months. He reminded me of the deal: "Complete Teen Challenge and I will send you to the college of your choice."

I felt I could last four more months. Dave Wilkerson was happy and Jay was happy. The staff on duty was happy, so they sent me back to my cabin. At about 1:00 a.m., I was awakened and brought to Dave Kirschke's office.

He was not happy. "If you stay here, you stay for me, not Wilkerson. I run the program and I tell you what you can do and when you can leave. If I say you need to be here two years to fulfill your covenant with God, you're here two years. So what will it be, trust me with your life or leave now and rebel against God?"

Two hours later, I was hitchhiking on Highway 59, praying I wasn't going to hell. I wasn't out there long before a car sped by me, turned around, and picked me up. Playing on his car stereo was "Fly like an Eagle" by the Steve Miller Band. I asked the driver where he was headed and with a satanic snigger, he said, "I'm going to hell just like you."

Although the Steve Miller Band is still one of my favorite bands, I still can't listen to that song. Thankfully, the ride was short and I wasted no time in praying, "God was this a sign that I needed to go back? If that was true then let them find me, I'm willing to go back."

I looked up and saw the Teen Challenge van pull alongside me. I was so happy. God was still speaking to me. God thought enough of me to send the Teen Challenge van out to rescue me from the petrifying prospect of going to hell. I told Bobby, the van driver, and one of my Bible teachers how happy I was to see them and that I'd like to come back and start all over again.

Bobby informed me, "We're not here to bring you back. We think you stole some books from the library, open your suitcase, and dump it on the side of the road."

They looked at my stuff thrown along Highway 59 and found no stolen books. Heartbroken I asked, "Does this mean I don't get to go back and undo what I did? Does this mean I'm going to hell?"

Bobby shook his head and left me to repack my suitcase.

I stood there in disbelief and sadness. It seemed that God had really cast me out of His Kingdom because I couldn't submit to someone else's authority. Was there any hope of me walking with God or was I eternally damned? I do not remember having begged God for a sign since I had been on Route 66 nine years ago, but that morning I pleaded, "God, please help me to know what way I am supposed to be traveling? I am still willing to go back to Teen Challenge, but it doesn't seem like you want me to go there. God, if I am heading in the right direction, please let the next ride offer me something to eat."

I should have asked God for something bigger: the next ride was very brief, but the driver offered me a hamburger.

When I got out of the car, I remember thinking, "God that was really nice but perhaps I needed to ask you for a sign that would be less likely to be seen as a coincidence."

My thoughts continued, "God please let the next ride talk to me about Jesus before I say a word."

It didn't seem long before a car stopped that had a Jesus bumper sticker on it. The driver, who identified himself as Michael Huff, said, "I've never done this before, but I need to tell you about Jesus." Excitedly, I told Michael my testimony.

After I told him my story, he drove me to Huntsville, Texas and invited me to stay with him. He got me a job at Casa Tomas Mexican restaurant as a waiter and then got me involved in his church, The First Baptist Church of Huntsville. I started believing that God wasn't done with me. After a year in Huntsville, I felt strong enough to return to my family in Haverhill.

# CHAPTER 26

*How quickly we forget God's great deliverances in our lives. How easily we take for granted the miracles he performed in our lives.*[66]

My original plan was to visit my mom and sister for two weeks and then return to Huntsville. One night I went to a Boston jazz club and sat in with the band. The owner of the club told me that if I was interested in performing there on a regular basis, he could introduce me to other musicians who would love to play with me. Eddy Ellis was born again, and Fred Shapiro cashed in the return trip ticket to Huntsville. Once again, jazz replaced Jesus as Lord.

One Sunday night on my way to work, I saw a sign that said "Tent Meeting featuring PTL TV speaker, Paul Slater."[67]

I had a couple of hours before my gig, so I slipped into the last row of the tent. I wasn't inspired by the service, so I decided to leave. As I rose from my seat, a man who introduced himself as Bob Craft (not the New England Patriot's owner) came over to me. I informed him that I had already accepted Jesus as my Savior, and I needed to go to work. He

---

[66] Dave Wilkerson
[67] The PTL Club (PTL stands for "Praise The Lord" or "People That Love"), was a Christian television program originally hosted by evangelists Jim and Tammy Faye Bakker, which ran from 1974 to 1989.

took my hand and put an envelope in it saying, "This is for you. Don't tell anyone."

By this time, Paul Slater had finished speaking and noticed me talking to Bob Craft. He came over to us and asked if I knew Jesus. I found myself telling him about what had happened at Teen Challenge and asked if he thought I was damned to hell.

He took my hand and said, "Not if you are ready to come back." I wept and once again recommitted my life to Jesus.

Before leaving, I met the pastor of the Assembly of God Church, Reverend Lamar Breazeale. I told him I had just recommitted my life to the Lord and then found myself asking the boldest question I had ever asked of anyone.

"Pastor, I don't want to see people backslide the way I've been doing and Haverhill has no Christian bookstore. May I start a Christian book table in the back of your church?" I had never met him or been to his church.

Reverend Breazeale looked at me and said, "Young man I don't know you and there's no way I would let you do that, except that Reverend Slater came up to me and said, 'That young man is going to ask you for something, I don't know what it is, but whatever it is, say 'yes'."

It was too late for me to get to the club, so before I left the church, I called the jazz club and told the band to start without me but that I was on my way. I then remembered Bob Craft's envelope, I opened it, and there was twice the amount of money that I would've earned had I gone to work. I used that money to start the book table.

There are many miracles connected with the ministry that began as a book table in the back of the Assembly of God Church, that I could write a book on that ministry alone. Four miracles continue to help me recognize God as my provider.

# CHAPTER 27

For the next two Sundays the book table completely sold out of books. One Sunday night, Pastor Breazeale invited me to come forward to be prayed over. During the prayer time, I had an overwhelming sense that God was about to do something gigantic in our community and in my life. When the prayer was over, I noticed only Wendy sitting in the audience.

Wendy approached me and invited me to join her, her mother, a guy named Bill, and several other people for coffee at a nearby restaurant. That night I discovered that Bill had been a disciple of Tony Alamo, the Hollywood evangelist I met when I first came to Hollywood. I also discovered that Wendy had worked in a Christian bookstore. By the end of the night, Wendy convinced me that if we had just a bit more money, the book table could evolve into a bookstore. Wendy had a little bit of money and so did Bill. The three of us became partners.

The following day, Wendy and I drove throughout Haverhill looking for the ideal storefront. There seemed to be nothing available. On the way to Wendy's home, we drove through West Newbury and stopped for dinner at the West Newbury House of Pizza.

In my youth, West Newbury was a rural farming town. Because of its favorable location, West Newbury, has been transformed in the past ten years into one of the most affluent communities in Essex County.[68]

While waiting for our meal, we noticed a GOING OUT OF BUSINESS sign on a Christian bookstore next to the restaurant. Stelios, the owner of the restaurant, informed us that the bookstore owner was offering the inventory and displays at a very good price. We were excited but knew that the cost of the space in this community was more than we could possibly afford.

As Stelios served us our pizza, he asked what the name of the store would be. We thought that a Christian store that reflected my Jewish heritage would be unique, and we thought about Yerushalayem West.

Stelios laughed and said, "That name will be very difficult for people to remember."

As he said that, a woman at the counter turned around said excitedly, "The name means Jerusalem West and I think it's a beautiful name."

That woman asked if she could join us for dinner. Carol was not only friends with the bookstore owner, but was a strong supporter of Jews for Jesus. We agreed to meet Carol at the bookstore the following morning.

Carol was already there when we arrived the next morning. She had already written checks to the bookstore owner as well as to Stelios. Yerushalayem West opened two weeks later.

We hoped that Yerushalayem West would be more than a bookstore. Our vision was for a bookstore–coffeehouse. We sent out invitations to local and national Christian singers and bands to perform on Saturday nights. The first band to respond to our invitation was The Liberated Wailing Wall, the Jews for Jesus musical team from San Rafael.

---

[68] In 2006, Essex County received the dubious honor of being named number one on Forbes magazine's list of most overpriced places to live in the U.S. due to its high living costs and expensive real estate.

# CHAPTER 28

As soon as The Liberated Wailing Wall came to Yerushalayem West, other singers and bands wanted to play there. Bill Ellis, Richard Johnson, Tom and Peppy Petrovsky, and Celestial Forge are just a handful of the musicians who helped make Yerushalayem West become a special place every Saturday night. After the music, I would share a brief evangelistic message.

One night an area couple named John and Ann Woods came to the coffeehouse and came to know Jesus as Savior. Soon John left his job at the Seabrook Nuclear plant, enrolled in Gordon-Conwell Theological Seminary, and became a minister in the United Church of Christ.

The bookstore and ministry was great, but little money was coming in. To help pay expenses, I took a job delivering the Boston Globe newspaper. I also took a job driving a taxi. My driving career was put on hold when someone went through a red light and plowed into my taxi. I suffered the usual whiplash and a few bruises, but I was OK.

While I was recuperating, Wendy took a job as a sales clerk while I watched the store. Financially, things weren't looking great. Thankfully, now and then, I had the opportunity to preach in local churches. One of these churches in Peabody, Massachusetts, was pastored by Warren Hyam. Pastor Warren helped me recognize that God was supernaturally keeping the doors of our ministry open.

I preached there one Sunday and forgot my glasses on the podium. Warren came down the following day to return them. After I apologized to him for having to drive all the way up from Peabody, he asked me how he could help our bookstore–ministry.

I laughed and asked, "You don't happen to have $475 on you do you? Our rent is due today."

Warren said, "Now I know why a total stranger came by this morning and gave me this envelope." In the envelope was $500.

# CHAPTER 29

God kept sending us special messengers like Warren Hyam, Les Carroll, John Woods, Carol Climo, Shirley Jacques, and Frank Hobbs, to encourage us to stay faithful. One night in prayer, I sensed that we should plan a Memorial Day event at a nearby lake that would be called "Day in the Son". This would feature bands, speakers, and food. This would be the third miracle.

Everything fell into place quickly. The town issued permits for the lakefront. We arranged the staging and sound, and we obtained permission to use the canoes. There was no stopping us.

The day before the festival, the weatherman announced a severe storm warning for Memorial Day. That Sunday evening, the phone calls came in asking if the event was cancelled. I told everyone that it was too early to tell, but I would make the call early in the morning. By 6:00 a.m., torrential rains had come, and a group of frustrated musicians, stagehands, and friends were at our storefront.

"Fred, it's unsafe to set up in this storm, you need to postpone the event!"

I lost it. I threw everyone out of the store, fell to the floor, and cried, "God, how could you treat us this way? For five months we've been planning this. All our plans had come together so nicely. If this wasn't your will how could it have developed the way it did?"

I felt God say, "It couldn't have."

Then I sensed that somehow this would be a greater "Day in the Son" than we could've imagined. As I lay on the floor, an inspiration came to me.

I called everyone, "What's the first thing we need to do at the lake?"

A stage person said, "The stage needs to go up, but its raining way too hard to do that." I then instructed the stage crew to go to the festival site, which was about five miles away. "When you get there if the rain has subsided enough to start putting up the stage, call and say we're putting up the stage. If you feel that you can't put up the stage, call and tell us that."

He called back a half hour later saying, "It's easing up enough for us to put up the stage. I'll call when we're done."

I called the person who handled the sound system. "Has the rain eased up enough for you to set up the sound equipment?"

The soundman had reservations about it, so I gave him the instructions that I had given to the staging guy: "Go to the site, when you get there, if you feel safe to set up the sound equipment do it, otherwise let me know, and I'll call the event off."

They arrived at the site and once again, by the time they got there, the rain had subsided enough for them to start setting up the sound equipment.

Some of the bands and speakers did cancel; however, by 10:00 a.m., Bill Ellis kicked off the festival. As he sang, the sun came out of the clouds, and by 1:00 p.m., boats and canoes filled the lake. A "Day in the Son" was an incredible display of God's provisions. Over the next four years, the Memorial Day event would include national artists like Larry Norman and Mike Warnke.

# CHAPTER 30

After a year and a half in West Newbury, I sensed it was time to change our location, so I gave Stelios three-month' notice. Wendy and I felt that the ministry belonged in Haverhill, not West Newbury. Our partner, Bill, disagreed and distanced himself from the ministry. For over two months, I scoured the paper for rentals and drove through areas that I felt called for ministry. There was nothing available. On the Wednesday before our scheduled Saturday move, the mover called asking for an address where to move everything. I said, "When I know you'll know." It was at that moment that depression really set in. Why had I foolishly told the landlord we were moving? I couldn't see how we would find a place in just three days. Once again we really needed a miracle.

That night, while Wendy and I were visiting my mom, I happened to glance at her newspaper. An ad for a storefront jumped out at me. I called the number, and the owner of the property said, "I am leaving for Florida at 7:00 a.m. tomorrow, but I can meet you at the store at 4:00 a.m.

It was early, but I was there! He was there! On Saturday, we moved just two blocks away from the statue of Hannah Dustin scalping the Abenaki Indians. While we were unpacking, Linda, one of our most faithful supporters from West Newbury, came in.

"Linda, how did you know where we were moving to?" I asked.

"I didn't even know you had moved, but I happen to live upstairs, right over your store."

My heart leaped. God had provided this location, so we changed the name to God's Provision. While at our former store-coffee house, if we saw people waiting at the door when we arrived to open up, we knew they were customers. At God's Provision in Haverhill, we knew the people at the door were hookers and dealers. From the outset, we realized that by moving from West Newbury to White Street in Haverhill, we would no longer be serving a comfortable affluent community. We were unaware of the spiritual battles that we would actually face.

It was not an uncommon event for street gangs to drop off people at our door in the middle of the night, knowing that we would take them to the hospital. Occasionally, undercover cops or agents used our store as an observation post to watch for criminals and arrest them. Thanks to responsive reporters at the Lawrence Eagle Tribune and Haverhill Gazette, God's Provision eventually became off-limits to the police for this activity.

Some highpoints of our three-year miracle in Haverhill included the following:

- Hosted Thanksgiving and Christmas banquets for over 200 people, including a banquet and gifts for the children. This children's event was featured on WCVB Channel 5 and earned us commendations by the Massachusetts Senate, House of Representatives, and the City of Haverhill.
- Saw persons with substance abuse and life controlling issues enter into rehab programs and even colleges.
- Inspired churches to develop outreach programs for the hungry, homeless, and destitute. For example, a local church took over our holiday meal program.

Although God was still using us to plant seeds in Haverhill, I still felt something was missing. I thought we needed a new vision, and Wendy seemed to agree with me.

# CHAPTER 31

I had met Dan Russell (president of New Sound) five years earlier when I worked for Preview Magazine. He had contacted me about taking out ads for an Andy Pratt concert that he was promoting in Boston.[69] After talking with him, I discovered that he had been Larry Norman's friend and part of his management team.

Dan contracted with us at God's Provision to sell CDs at all the New Sound events. He thought that the music retail arm of God's Provision needed a new name and thus New Vision Music was born. Once again, music was making its way to the foreground of my life, replacing the call that had given birth to and sustained my ministry.

The more time I spent with Dan and the artists he was bringing in, the more I wanted to work with music promotion again. I was convinced that my knowledge of and passion for Christian music was the one thing I possessed that would make a difference for God while helping me make a living.

In 1986, New Vision Music merged with New Sound. God's Provision was abandoned. Wendy and I moved to Chelsea, Massachusetts, where we were married. I enjoyed life in our new surroundings. I didn't miss

---

[69] Rolling Stone once praised Andy Pratt as "reviving the dream of rock as an art and then re-inventing it." He currently lives in the Netherlands and has recorded over twenty studio albums.

ministering to the hungry and homeless. I was enjoying working as manager of the New Sound System retail outlet alongside of Dan, his fiancée Alison, and his brother Joel. I was also enjoying the opportunity to sit in with the jazz musicians from Berklee College of Music.

It was a different story for Wendy. She missed God's Provision. It was not long before she left New Vision and began working as a clerk at the Massachusetts State House. In February, Wendy informed me that she was pregnant.

While Joseph was growing inside her, I felt that our life together in Chelsea was not growing. New Vision Music was not pulling its weight in the New Sound System. This was, in part, due to location, my lack of expertise as a store manager, and to the mail order companies' ability to deliver the same product within days at considerable discounts.

By the summer of 1987, Dan suggested strongly that I begin praying about a new calling and a new job. As I began to pray and talk with others, it became increasingly clear to me that I really wanted to be a pastor, which meant going to seminary. This seemed impossible; I had never finished college.

One night Margaret, the wife of the minister who had married Wendy and me, told me about Bangor Theological Seminary, a seminary in Maine that would accept non-college graduates if they agreed to get their bachelor degree within seven years after graduating. Wendy and I drove to Bangor, Maine, where I applied to the seminary. I was accepted and was eager to start the courses that would begin in September.

One week before classes were to begin, I received a call from the financial aid director. I was no longer eligible for financial aid because I had defaulted on my college loans. I called Point Loma and they gave me the number of the agency that was collecting my debt. I owed $20,000, but if I could pay within two days, they would settle for $7,000. I don't remember what Wendy did, but I wept. I was about to be a husband and father who felt once again had lost God's call, again.

That night, I received a call from a lawyer asking if I remembered him. He said three years ago he represented me in the accident where a driver had gone through a red light and smashed into my taxi. The driver and insurance company had finally agreed to settle. The amount of the settlement was $8,000.

The next day I paid off the college debt. With the remaining $1,000, I placed a first and last month's deposit on an apartment. The following Monday, I began life at Bangor Theological Seminary.

# CHAPTER 32

*There is no room in love for fear. Well-formed love banishes fear. Since fear is crippling, a fearful life—fear of death, fear of judgment—is one not yet fully formed in love* [70]

The day before I left for Bangor, I received a call from the First Baptist Church of Chelsea. They informed me that the front page of the Boston Globe had an article about the church and homosexuality, quoting a Bangor Seminary professor. I ran out, bought the paper, and saw a picture of Dr. Burton Throckmorton, with the following quote:

*"There is no reason. I can see why the church can't add to its scripture and delete from its scripture. I think the church can do with the scripture what it wants to do with the scripture."*

The article went on to say Throckmorton had appeared on the CBS This Morning show and The Phil Donahue Show in support of a translation of scripture that welcomed and affirmed homosexuality. I was a born-again Evangelical who spoke in "tongues" and believed in casting out demons. How could I possibly take a class from this liberal? I made up my mind I would not take a class from him while at Bangor.

---

[70] First John 4:18 as translated by Eugene Peterson in The Message, Nav Press Publishing company.

When I chose my classes, I discovered that his course on the New Testament was required. The first day of class, Dr. Throckmorton announced that there would be no tests and no attendance taken; our grade was dependent on a fifty-page paper submitted on a topic of our choice. I was afraid, really afraid, but I had a greater fear than Dr. Throckmorton's class.

Two months after arriving in Bangor, Joseph Barson Shapiro was born. Someone once said, "Fear is a tornado in the rear view mirror." I looked in the rear view mirror of my life and saw someone who didn't know what it was like to have a father. I was never taught how to throw a baseball or dribble a basketball. In that rearview mirror I saw someone who had been taunted and bullied throughout his youth. I saw someone who was afraid to fight. Indeed, the bravest thing I had ever done was to run away from the two Processeans at the Grateful Dead show sixteen years earlier, and hop into a cab. What could I possibly pass on to that beautiful boy in Wendy's arms?

I wanted to say to him, "Joe, just look at me and do the exact opposite of everything I do, and you'll be just fine."

I tried to step outside the Eastern Maine Medical Center for a cigarette, but I couldn't move. I became paralyzed and was afraid that if I stepped outside, the moon was going to fall and hit me in the head. Joseph deserved so much more than I could offer him.

I went back upstairs to hold him in my arms. It was like holding a burning candle, hard to hold but so, so beautiful to experience.

Being Joe's father has been the hardest yet most meaningful and celebratory aspect of my life. Joe brings more happiness to me than I've ever deserved to experience. Someone once said, "Love is a robot that's learned to feel." Joe is still teaching me how to feel.

# CHAPTER 33

*"Passion, incredible erudition and above all the depth of faith cultivated by a life in and for the church: that is Burton Throckmorton*[71]

Life was not easy that first semester in the seminary. I had never been a good student. Now I was a husband and a father, too. I was also working two jobs. The pressure was a balloon filling inside me, ready to burst.

I struggled with church history, theology, ethics, and pastoral care, but I was surprisingly excited by what I learned from the one person that I feared the most.

Burton Throckmorton had been teaching New Testament for sixty years and was a protégé of Rudolf Bultmann, translating Bultmann's commentary on the Gospel of John into English.[72]

Before Throckmorton came to Bangor, he had taught at Union Theological Seminary, Columbia University, and Princeton University.

---

[71] Susan Brooks Thistlethwaite, past president of Chicago Theological Seminary, in her review of Burton Throckmorton's "Jesus Christ, The Message of the Gospels, The Hope of the Church" (1989, Westminster John Knox Press).

[72] Rudolf Karl Bultmann was a German Lutheran theologian and professor of New Testament at the University of Marburg. He was one of the major figures of early 20th century biblical studies and a prominent voice in neo-orthodox Christianity.

He had studied at the Juilliard School and for two years was on Broadway with Shirley Booth and Van Johnson in Sunday Nights with Joan.

His *Gospel Parallels* has been used as a text for sixty years in most theological schools throughout the country. Burton Throckmorton's presence challenged every aspect of my personhood. This man had been to Juilliard and appeared on Broadway. I couldn't even brag about my singing to him.

At the end of the semester, I had received a C in ethics and B- in both church history and theology. The Dean of the Seminary, Dr. Dickhaut, gave me a D in Pastoral Care and even questioned why I came to the seminary. While standing in the seminary commons weeping, Dr. Throckmorton saw me. "Mr. Shapiro I was just going to deliver your grade to your mailbox but I might as well give it to you. Are you crying? What is the matter, may I help?"

I shared with him what the Dean had said and my own doubts about the seminary. He smiled and said, "Before you do anything rash, take a look at the grade I gave you. You were the only A+ in the class. I will talk to Dr. Dickhaut and get that D changed for you. Please don't quit, you have a brilliant mind, and you are my favorite fundamentalist."

I don't have a brilliant mind, and I'm not a fundamentalist, but I do serve a God of miracles. Dr. Dickhaut met with me and changed my grade. The next class I took with him, I got an A. At Bangor, I discovered that God could use a liberal scholar to inspire a Jew for Jesus.

My relationship with Burton Throckmorton turned things around in the seminary but not in my marriage. In February of 1990, Wendy and I separated. Her mother came to pick her and Joe up in a U-Haul. Perhaps the saddest moment of my life was seeing Joe standing outside of his grandma's car and asking, "Grandma, why is Da[73] crying?" His

---

[73] Joe picked up the name da from the 1988 film about a playwright who relives memories with his father (Da).

grandmother slowly looked at me and then at him and said, "He should be crying," and I still am.

If things seemed hard before, they seemed impossible now. I was afraid there would be no pigs flying in the future of a divorced, Jewish, overweight Charismatic follower of Rudolf Bultmann who still lisped. My fears were confirmed at the American Baptist Churches Biennial in Charleston, West Virginia.

At an interview, an executive minister from the South smiled at me and said, "You've got three things going against you from ever being a pastor at a church in the South: number one, you are Jewish; number two, you're going through a divorce; and number three, you're a Yankee."

Even Dr. Throckmorton advised me to pursue a career in teaching and not a career as a pastor. Nevertheless, there were four people who believed in my pastoral call. First, Reverend Dr. Louis George, my Baptist polity professor, kept assuring me that in the right church, God could use me in a big way. Second, Dr. Rex Garrett, the director of the chaplain intern program at Eastern Maine Medical Center, convinced me that I could live with my shadows and sins and still live as a healing presence. Third, Reverend Charlie Dorchester, a retired Methodist minister and member of the Kenduskeag Union Church, the church that I pastored as a student.

Reverend Dorchester kept affirming me as one of the best preachers he had ever heard. Thirteen years down the road, we would meet again.

Finally, and unexpectedly, there was Busch Pelletier, leader of a band called Bushwhack. One night Bushwhack was playing in Bangor. I attended and was surprised to see David, a Berklee keyboardist who I had played with in the Boston area. He introduced me to Busch. Once a month Bushwhack came to the Bangor Singles Club on a Saturday night, and I never missed them. Dr. George, Dr. Garrett, Reverend Dorchester, and Busch inspired me to finish my degree at Bangor and move toward ordination.

Upon graduating, Reverend Dorchester asked me to stay on and pastor the Kenduskeag Union Church while waiting for a full-time church. I declined and decided to leave Maine and move back home to Haverhill. There, I could be closer to my son and my mom. Maybe I could even patch my relationship with Wendy. My mom's husband Bob had died, so she invited me to live with her. Of course, I did. While living in Haverhill, I preached at the First Baptist Church of East Boston.

One night while returning from preaching at the church, I noticed a sign at Trader Alan's Truck Stop that said the Monday night jam session was featuring Bushwhack. I showed up at the truck stop that Monday night. It was crowded with truckers and hookers. I was sure all of them used drugs. Busch introduced me as Reverend Fred. He also introduced me to Patrick, the restaurant manager, and that night I began working the graveyard shift as a waiter or dishwasher.

My first year out of seminary was tough. As other graduates were finding full-time church positions, I was waiting on tables, washing dishes, and singing songs in a truck stop. It was a year before a Grafton County, New Hampshire church would call me to pastor their church. My recommendations from Rex Garrett and Lou George had been so impressive that all they needed was a tape of me preaching. Of course, I had no tape.

When I asked Busch if he'd be willing to bring some recording equipment to East Boston, he said, "I have a better idea. Preach here at the truck stop. We'll pack the house. I'll make signs telling people when to laugh and say Amen. It will be great. A live tape will be much better."

It was a memorable evening. The taping went great. The church loved the tape and called me to be their pastor. Wendy did not want to go to New Hampshire. She stayed in Haverhill, and we agreed to divorce. My divorce from Wendy and subsequent knowledge that I would no longer see Joe on a daily basis robs any other painful experience I've ever been through of its sting. For the next two years, the highlight of my weekday would be the 5:00 p.m. phone call to Joe as we watched Goof Troop together.

# CHAPTER 34

*Heaven have mercy on us all-Presbyterians and Pagans alike-for we are all somehow dreadfully cracked about the head and sadly need mending*[74]

*To the last I grapple with thee; from hell's heart I stab at thee; for hate's sake I spit my last breath at thee*[75]

Zaydah's favorite movie was *Moby Dick*. We saw it at the Paramount Theater when I was seven years old and afterwards. I went right out to buy the classic's illustrated comic version of the novel. I still wonder whom Zaydah identified with in Moby Dick. Was it Moby Dick himself—a white-headed whale with a wrinkled brow and a crooked jaw? Was it Captain Ahab who loses his leg to Moby Dick, goes insane, and blames the whale for all of the evil ever since time began?

Ahab hid his insanity well. Ahab acted like a sane man, but his motives were insane. He accepted the calling of captain only to pursue his personal obsession. Melville describes Ahab as a monomaniac, one who obsesses on a single thing and, more importantly, is only insane when it comes to that one thing.

---

[74] Herman Melville "Moby Dick"
[75] Ibid Ahab's last words

There's a monomaniac in the Bible also named Ahab. The similarity between the two Ahab's is strong. King Ahab would've been a great king if it weren't for his obsession with the idol worshipper Jezebel. Captain Ahab would've been a great captain if it weren't for his obsession with Moby Dick. Just as King Ahab's obsession with Jezebel dooms all of Israel, Captain Ahab's obsession with Moby Dick dooms his ship.

At the book's end, Ahab hurls his last harpoon into Moby Dick's flesh but becomes tangled in the harpoon's rope. Ahab is killed by own twisted obsession and Moby Dick ultimately destroys Ahab's crew.

Moby Dick's Ahab was a Quaker. He sought revenge in spite of his religion. As I reflect on my last twenty-five years of pastoral ministry, the story of the two Ahab's scares me. Am I driven by my past as they were? Is my calling governed by my religion or my obsession with acceptance and affirmation? Is it possible that I've learned from Hannah Dustin, how to use my Bible as a tomahawk to kill sleeping Christians? Have I destroyed more churches than I've delivered?

In February 1991, I arrived in the Grafton County church. I was greeted by enthusiastic diaconates who were cleaning, furnishing, and beautifying my new home, the parsonage. The deacons wanted to make sure that their pastor, recently separated from his wife, was well cared for so he could concentrate on the teaching and preaching of God's Word.

The first thing that Bertha, a deacon, and one of the oldest members of the church, asked me to do was sign a covenant that promised I would not allow single woman into the parsonage after 8:00 p.m. She told me it was for my own good. Bertha had an unshakeable sense of herself as good, right, and saved. She put a lot of energy into reminding others of the eternal torments awaiting those less good, less right, and less saved than she was. Bertha and the other deacons kept tighter tabs on me than a guard would to a death row inmate.

Nightly, they would drive by the parsonage, park in the lot adjacent to the senior housing complex next door, and watch me. They watched when I would leave, when I would return, and whom I might return with. The surveillance was increased by a shut-in named Ruth who lived at the apartment complex and whose living room window faced my back door. Next to her window, she kept a pair of high-powered binoculars. Ruth was the first person to phone me when there were doubting deacons watching.

In hindsight, these boundaries probably kept me safer and contributed to my ability to grow the church, for the church did grow quickly. Unfortunately, all of their reconnaissance and boundaries could not protect me or the church from JQ who visited the church after the Concord Monitor did a story on our resurgence.

JQ was not beautiful, but she was so self-assured that she was one of the most captivating women I had ever met. That night she bewitched the deacons with her singing, her sophistication, and her religious background. The head deacon seemed so taken with her that he acted as if her voice could bring world peace.

After the service, he not only invited her to sing the next Sunday morning, but he slipped $20 into my hands and encouraged me to take her out to dinner. At dinner, she informed me that her grandfather was a Methodist bishop who in 1948 had been on the cover of Time Magazine. I really wanted to know more about JQ.

The next day, she asked if she could accompany me to an American Baptist luncheon meeting. She had everyone dripping like John the Baptist. One executive assured me, "If you stick with her, you'll end up at Riverside Church in New York." Everyone who met her agreed that she was a keeper.

After that day, JQ and I spent just about every day together. She seemed as excited about my upcoming installation service as I was.[76]

---

[76] After a period of about 3-6 months, a local American Baptist Church holds an installation in order to celebrate the calling of the pastor and clarify the responsibility the pastor has toward the church. Invited to the service are friends and family of the pastor, friends and family of church members,

When my robe did not arrive in time for the installation, she offered me her grandfather's robe. It not only fit, but it was the same color that I had ordered. She zipped the robe, kissed me softly, and said, "I am your miracle."

My mom arrived at the house that night for the installation and at dinner, I discovered that she needed a miracle more than I did. A group of our friends went out to eat with us and at least five times Mom asked to go home and take care of her garden. She kept asking whether she had remembered to buy her lottery ticket. When she returned from the women's room, she ended up at the wrong table.

Finally, she complained of an awful headache. Bertha suggested that she should take Mom home with her so that I could stay with my dinner guests. I never remembered seeing Mom that way before—neither could any of our friends. Everyone worried that it was the beginning of Alzheimer's disease. JQ had never met my mom, but she was passionate about me putting her into a home right away.[77]

The lights had gone off in my world, and my installation service was only a dim memory. I've been told that JQ's singing was the highlight. Other than what happened to Mom, I remember only one detail of the installation weekend.

Later that night, JQ told me how good I looked in her grandfather's robe and then added, "I need to confess, I've worn that robe in ceremonies, too."

"JQ, I didn't know you were a minister?"

"I'm not, I'm a witch, and I've worn the robe during WICCAN ceremonies."[78]

---

area pastors and denominational officials.

[77] A year later, mom was diagnosed with Alzheimer's, but her headache and forgetfulness disappeared the next day. She continued to live in her home for twelve more years and then finally moved to a nursing home in 2003

[78] Wicca is a modern pagan, witchcraft religion developed in England and

At first, I felt as if Bobby Mozzolla had punched me in the gut. Then I laughed and said, "You've got to be kidding."

She laughed and said, "Maybe one day I'll show you."

The following week, JQ, Chrissy who was a mutual friend from church, and I went for lunch. There was a boy at a nearby table eating chocolate ice cream. I noticed that JQ had closed her eyes.

I asked, "What's the matter?"

She replied, "I'm on a diet so I'm making that boy's ice cream taste bad."

The boy stopped eating and said to his mom, "This ice cream tastes like poop."

JQ smiled, and a chill came over my soul. I didn't want to see JQ too much after that day, but Chrissy did. Chrissy, who used to come over the house every night to play Nintendo Monopoly, started doing more things with JQ.

One night, JQ and Chrissy were sitting in church together when a person who claimed to have prophetic gifts was the guest speaker. As he walked around the room pointing at, touching, and sometimes yelling at the congregation, he walked over to JQ and Chrissy and said, "You two have a wonderful and powerful connection." JQ and Chrissy gazed into each other's eyes, held each other's hand, and smiled. Soon afterwards, Chrissy left her husband and entered into a short but influential relationship with JQ.

I never saw JQ after that night. Chrissy stopped attending church or Bible study regularly. A year later, however, Chrissy and I did help arrange for Superman's funeral.

---

introduced to the public in 1954 by Gerald Gardner. It draws upon a diverse set of ancient pagan and 20th century motifs for its structure and rituals

Some of you may remember that in 1992, in the Superman comic book series, Superman fought Doomsday in the streets of Metropolis. At the end of the fight, both Superman and Metropolis lay dead.[79]

Members of our Chamber of Commerce, on a lark, thought it might be good for business if the town could become known as Superman's final resting place. Chrissy and I made the arrangements and borrowed a hearse from the local funeral parlor. As the hearse rode along Main St, I was seen comforting the weeping Lois Lane (Chrissy). Bertha and the other deacons saw us and were aghast that their pastor would officiate at the funeral of a cartoon character.

A week after Superman's funeral, I married NB, a woman I had met a year earlier while officiating at the wedding of her son. Although the deacons were upset by my actions at Superman's funeral, they all came to our wedding. However, while in Boston on our honeymoon, the deacons secretly cut my salary in half. They had gotten even with me for the mock funeral.

Faster than a speeding bullet, my life in the Grafton County church was over. JQ heard the news, called, and managed to convince me that I was some kind of Superman, and that I wouldn't have to wait long for a new church calling. She was right; in a matter of weeks, I was asked to pastor a church in Vermont. It was there that I really discovered my kryptonite.

---

[79] Superman (vol. 2) #75 1992.

# CHAPTER 35

*"And you gave them kingdoms . . . And they captured fortified cities and a rich land, and took possession of houses full of all good things, cisterns already hewn, vineyards, olive orchards and fruit trees in abundance. So they ate and were filled and became fat and delighted themselves in your great goodness. Nevertheless, they were disobedient and rebelled against you and cast your law behind their back and killed your prophets, who had warned them in order to turn them back to you, and they committed great blasphemies. Therefore you gave them into the hand of their enemies, who made them suffer. And in the time of their suffering they cried out to you and you heard them from heaven, and according to your great mercies you gave them saviors who saved them from the hand of their enemies. But after they had rest they did evil again before you, and you abandoned them to the hand of their enemies, so that they had dominion over them. Yet when they turned and cried to you, you heard from heaven, and many times you delivered them according to your mercies. And you warned them in order to turn them back to your law. Yet they acted presumptuously . . . Therefore you gave them into the hand of the peoples of the lands. Nevertheless, in your great mercies you did not make an end of them or forsake them, for you are a gracious and merciful God. Nehemiah 9:22-31 (ESV)*

How merciful is God? This Jewish legend attempts to answer.

A man had a young son who was stricken with a mysterious illness. Each day the little boy grew weaker. The man sensed the angel of death hovering over his son and needed a miracle.

He went to a tzadik who tried his best to cure the boy. The tzadik finally said, "There's nothing I can do. It's been decreed that the Gates of Heaven remain locked to your only son." The man pleaded for him to try again, and the old tzadik said he would make one more attempt.

As he prayed and fasted, the tzadik had an idea. He summoned his young assistant and asked him to find ten hardened criminals and bring them to his home. The assistant thought this was crazy but his respect for the tzadik was so profound, he obeyed without questioning.

The assistant found ten thieves and was amazed at how readily they agreed to accompany him. At the tzadik's home, each criminal tried to outdo the others by bragging about his most infamous crime.

Finally, the tzadik told them to quiet down and pray. He commanded such respect that they became quiet and listened to how they could participate in this difficult miracle. They did exactly what he told them to do. The next day the mystic learned the little boy had a miraculous recovery. "It's as though he was never sick!" his father said.

The assistant was puzzled and asked the tzadik, "Why didn't you ask for God-fearing, upstanding citizens? Why did you pray with such shady characters?" The mystic smiled, "A thief knows about breaking and entering. They can pick locks. They picked the celestial lock and broke into Heaven. That is how my prayers broke into the Heavenly Sanctuary."

Do you see it? The tzadik in this story represents our gifts, talents, and strengths. The tzadik represents everything that is good about us. Conversely, the thieves represent our negative qualities. Our thieves are all of the stuff that pinpoint us as sinners. The thieves represent everything in us that inspires God to come after us. Maybe that's why that it is only in darkness that we see the brightest Light.

There was a lot of excitement when my new wife and I arrived in Montpelier, Vermont. Dr. George had once told me that I would shine in a church that needed specialized ministry. When I asked what kind of church that was, he shook his head saying, "It wasn't in Grafton County, but it may be Montpelier."

My ministry in Montpelier did start off with a bang. The first year was staggering—the scarce were transformed into the scores. The Sunday morning church quartet grew into a gospel choir of sixty people. One night the church was so celebratory that the cops came by to see what was happening.[80] That night trustees worried that the floor would collapse. I was finally feeling like Superman until suddenly I crashed into clumps of kryptonite.

Just three weeks after my ordination, complaints from both older and newer members reached Dr. George simultaneously. Up till that moment, I had blamed lots of people for the complications and crises in our church. I had blamed the old church members for not welcoming and accepting people from the outside who were after the new life that Jesus promised. I had blamed younger church members for hastily and impatiently desiring to break from the music, traditions, and rituals of the older members.

I had even blamed the denomination, but I can't remember why. What I do remember was that less than a month after my ordination, I was agreeing to a week of emotional and vocational testing in Boston where a team would evaluate whether I was fit to pastor. The Commission on Ministry ultimately concluded that although I was fit to pastor, I would benefit from training in pastoral counseling. I applied to the doctoral program in Family System's Counseling at Eastern Baptist Seminary in

---

[80] As of 2013, the Montpelier Community Gospel Choir, under the direction of John Harrison, is still inspiring audiences and has performed with artists like Fontella Bass, David Krauss and Tammy Fletcher.

Philadelphia and was accepted. For the next three years I would spend one month a year in Philadelphia while working with a local mentor in my church.

During the assessment, I was gripped by the revelation that I had been ditching duty and abandoning answerability all of my life. I had hidden from Bobby Mozzolla, played hooky from school, had been suspended from two colleges, fled from family and friends, quit Jews for Jesus, hightailed it out of Hungerford, Texas, Teen Challenge, walked out of the Church of the Open Door, and away from God's Provision. In seminary, I sacrificed my wife and son, and now I was darting toward divorce once again. I finally saw why Dr. Dickhaut wanted to give me a D in pastoral care. He recognized I was not going to be able to commit myself to a church long enough to pastorally care for its members.

Indeed, in Grafton County, I spent more time preparing the funeral of a dead comic book hero than pastoring the people who had called me as their shepherd. Oh, I had always started things off with a bang, but I would speedily split once kryptonite exploded in my face. When would I stop scarpering and stand up and stay with the face being blasted by kryptonite?

As I left the evaluation, Dr. Ott, head of the evaluation team, hugged me and promised, "One day, you will quit running and stay with a church long enough to pastorally care for them, and both you and the church will experience overwhelming hurt when you have to leave."

As I headed North on Route 93, I begged God for another chance to confront kryptonite and thereby prove to God that I could demonstrate the supernatural power and mercy of God alive in my life. God was faithful. A week before my classes in Philadelphia were scheduled to begin, kryptonite crushed again— a team of oncologists concluded cancer was very much alive in my body.

# CHAPTER 36

*You can see a person's whole life in the cancer they get.*[81]

I had first noticed a tumor while pastoring in the Grafton County Church where I met JQ and buried Superman. One day it would be there, the next day it was gone. I had been analyzed, x-rayed, CAT scanned, and biopsied, with no conclusive results.

Buried

In 1993, a Jewish pathologist at Massachusetts General Hospital consulted with me. "Shapiro you have a strange name for a Baptist minister and even a stranger growth. I have no idea what it is. If it goes away, don't worry. Otherwise we'll do more tests."

It went away the next day, so I didn't worry about it. However, two years later, during the physical required for admission into Eastern Baptist Seminary, the tumor showed up again. This time it was diagnosed again as cancer. Treatments of chemotherapy and radiation were to begin as soon as my first month of the doctoral program was finished. I was challenged and inspired by all that I was learning, but my concern over the cancer screamed, shrieked, and yelled at me all month long.

---

[81] Haruki Murakami's short story "Blind Willow, Sleeping Woman"

*For Your Tomorrows*

Inexplicably, every sign of the cancer disappeared the day before chemo was to begin. I believed that I was healed. I called the oncologist to tell him the good news. He asked to see me.

After some tests he agreed, "Yes, the tumors have all appeared to shrink and I understand why you think that you're healed but I encourage you to still have the treatments. If you are healed, you've nothing to lose. However if the cancer is still there, the chemo and radiation will make a big difference."

The doctor left the office while my wife and I talked it over.

While he was out of the room, his nurse walked over to us and said, "I'm not telling you what to do, but if the same thing that happened to you happened to me, I would not go through the treatments."

Suddenly, I felt like I was driving in a fog bank. I couldn't see ahead of me or behind me. I was confused, uneasy, and nervous. Do I slow down or do I speed up? I couldn't think my way out of it. I let the oncologist think for me.

I sped up, racing through the fog bank, and did go through with the treatments. The cancer was gone and so was my hair and much of my hearing. I was told that chemo often causes hearing loss. For the next year, I had to listen close and try to read lips. Over the last twenty years, the cancer has come and gone five times. I wonder sometimes what would've happened had I listened to the nurse and slowed down in that fog bank.

# CHAPTER 37

*Some Christians believe we should never struggle with doubt, fear, anxiety, disillusionment, depression, sorrow, or agony. And when Christians do, it is because they're not exercising the quality of faith they ought to; periods of disillusionment and despair are sin. If those ideas are true, then I'm not a good Christian. Not only have I suffered physically with health problems, but I also spent a great deal of time struggling with depression during my battle with cancer.*[82]

Some of our friends in Montpelier had been visiting the Toronto Airport Christian Fellowship (a former Vineyard Church) and attested to remarkable miracles taking place. My wife and I flew out there to check it out.[83]

The opening worship music was perhaps the best I had ever heard. Suddenly, for whatever reason, a person's laughter erupted like a

---

[82] John Wimber co-founder of the Vineyard movement
[83] Rodney Howard-Browne, a South African minister associated with the Word-Faith Movement, is the recognized "Father" of holy laughter. He calls himself a "Holy Ghost Bartender," who thus dispenses the "new wine" of joy that leads to people being "drunk in the Spirit." The Association of Vineyard Churches has expelled the Airport Vineyard Fellowship from its association for "going over the edge" and is now trying to distance itself from it.

*For Your Tomorrows*

volcano. By the end of the worship segment, there were people barking like dogs, rolling on the carpet and laughing hysterically.

I began to laugh myself when an elder came and informed me that the spirit had given me the holy laughter. I laughed even harder after that, especially at the female Dutch preacher whose language I couldn't understand. I laughed a lot that night, but when we were not at the meetings, I cried a lot.

My second marriage was not surviving the church conflicts or the cancer. While in Toronto, my wife's angry words, side-looks, and imagined put-downs felt like Bobby Mozzolla's lead pipe crashing down on my head. Only God knows what pain I must've been inflicting on her. By the end of the week, we were spending our days apart. I had no intention of attending the service the last night. I was more interested in learning whether Susan Hawk or Richard Hatch would win Survivor on the TV.[84] Somehow, I ended up back at the church.

The female Dutch preacher had an interpreter, but I still couldn't understand a word she said. Somehow, my own diminished love for my wife, members of my church, and me was blocking out everything that the preacher was saying. Then in the midst of the sermon, for the first time in my life, I had an out-of-body experience.

I left my merciless, unloving, and judgmental body and hovered over it. I saw it for what it was. I also knew that in spite of everything, God still loved me. For the first time in my life, I knew why God valued a relationship with me.

---

[84] Survivor is a reality game show where contestants are isolated in the wilderness and compete for cash and other prizes. Each week contestants vote off other contestant until one final contestant remains. and wins the title of "Sole Survivor." Survivor: Borneo was the first season of the United States version of the show and after 39 days of competition was won by Richard Hatch. In 2006, it was revealed that Hatch failed to declare his winnings, among other earnings, in his tax return and was sentenced to 51 months imprisonment.

As I wept, my soul returned to my body. Now I heard the first words all night from the speaker whom I understood. She was talking to me. "Do you see how healthy you really are?"

I nodded my head and began to weep. The speaker asked, "Then why haven't you come forward?"

Many had come forward for healing, but she sent them back saying, "I'm not talking to you right now; I'm talking to a man who has lost his hearing."

As she said that, she signaled to her interpreter who walked up to me. I began to shake and weep. The speaker motioned to me to come forward. She covered my ears, prayed, and then pointed her finger at me. It was as if electricity filled my body. I fell backwards and landed on the floor.

When I was finally helped up, she turned me away from her and whispered, "Can you hear me?"

I did.

She moved further away and repeated the process. I heard every word. When I got home, I immediately drove down to see my son Joe who put me through the same test she did, and I heard every word.

My healing lasted for the next six months. I heard everything people said to me. Of course, that was longer than my marriage or my ministry in Vermont would last. My hearing slowly degraded. I now wear an aid in each ear.

After months of marital counseling, divorce seemed inevitable. Upon learning about the risk of our divorce, the deacons of the church met with me and suggested I resign. Thankfully, Dr. George still believed that one day I would discover the church that needed specialized ministry. He recommended me for the First Baptist Church of Milton, Massachusetts.

# CHAPTER 38

Both President George H. W. Bush and architect Buckminster Fuller were born in Milton. Milton also has the highest percentage (38%) of residents per capita, citing Irish heritage, of any town in the United States. None of that was important to me. What was important was that in my youth, my favorite place in the world was Milton, Massachusetts.

This was where much of my Zaydah's family lived. When I was twelve years old, I had my first real kiss in Milton. I lived for the Sundays when my Uncle Harry would drive us all down to Milton. Of course, once I became a Christian, my relationships with the Orthodox Jewish relatives in Milton were severed.

For twenty-seven years, I had no reason to go to Milton. Then I met Pablo Calzoncit, an area minister of The American Baptist Churches of Massachusetts, who was looking for someone to help revitalize a struggling church. He was totally convinced I could do this. I agreed to a three-year contract.

Thanks to the support of The American Baptist Churches of Massachusetts (TABCOM), the First Baptist Church of Milton grew during those three years. As a result of a weekly radio ministry on a Boston station and a weekly concert series in a local park, church attendance grew. Pablo himself became a member of the church and began calling the church the Milton Miracle. It is a miracle that someone who spent his life running from bullies and marriages, prematurely leaving schools and ministries, buried Superman, and dated a witch, held all these positions.

- TABCOM's Chair of the Board of Evangelism and Church Planting
- A member of the American Baptist Churches, Church Planters Institute
- A member of the General Board of the American Baptist Churches of the USA.

The paramount of miracles, however, was the 1999 All-Star Game.

# CHAPTER 39

*Baseball teaches us, or has taught most of us, how to deal with failure. We learn at a very young age that failure is the norm in baseball and, precisely because we have failed, we hold in high regard those who fail less often -- those who hit safely in one out of three chances and become star players. I also find it fascinating that baseball, alone in sports, considers errors to be part of the game, part of its rigorous truth.[85]*

Joe and I were in a toy store and as we were leaving, Joe noticed that we could sign up to win two tickets to the All-Star Game at Fenway Park. Because he was only twelve and couldn't win the contest, I entered. Not only did we win tickets to the game, we won tickets to three days of banquets, concerts, and All-Star activities, including limousine service and hotel accommodations. With all that, spending money was included.

How miraculous to sit at the same table as Jackie Robinson's widow? How miraculous to see Ted Williams? How miraculous to see Pedro Martinez strike out the first five of six batters he faced? How miraculous to see every one of the living nominees for the All-Century team? God moved powerfully in Milton!

Pablo eventually left to work in our national office, and I got a letter from the First Baptist Church of Willimantic, Connecticut.

---

[85] Francis T. Vincent, Jr., Commissioner of Baseball.

# CHAPTER 40

*"It is difficult to steer a parked car, so get moving."*[86]

In August 2003, I decided to drive down to Willimantic, Connecticut to meet with the search committee of the First Baptist Church. Before I left, TABCOM's Executive Minister gave me two warnings: leaving Massachusetts means you will no longer be on the Executive Board of American Baptist Churches and *60 Minutes* did a special on Willimantic, identifying it as "Heroin Town."

As I drove along Route 95, I ruminated about reasons to not leave Milton. I enjoyed being on the General Board of the American Baptist Churches. It is true that my presence didn't seem to profoundly impact the direction of our denomination, but I got pleasure from traveling to the conventions and occasionally having the opportunity to sing and speak in churches. I didn't feel called to pastor a church located in the center of what Dan Rather had called the Heroin Capital of the world. I had pretty much decided to stay in Milton until I saw a sign that said Route 66.

I'm used to seeing signs along Route 66. In the summer of 1971, it was a yellow Corvette. In the summer of 2003, it was four' 11' high bronze frogs who guard Willimantic's Frog Bridge which connects Route 66

---

[86] Henrietta Cornelia Mears . . .

and 32. I promise to tell the story about the frogs later but first, Zaydah's frog story.

Once upon a time, a tzadik on his death bed told his son, "Son, your mom and I are about to die. Mourn for the seven days and then go to the marketplace and purchase the first thing offered, no matter what it is, or whatever the cost. It will bring you good fortune just before the Passover." The son promised to obey.

The aged couple died that day and were buried together. After a week of mourning, the son and his wife made their way to the marketplace wondering what adventure was in store for them.

An old man with a silver casket of curious design approached.

"Purchase this, my son, and it will bring you good fortune."

"What does it contain?" asked the son.

"I can't tell you because I have never opened it. It cannot be opened until the feast which begins the Passover."

"What is the price?" the son asked.

"A thousand gold pieces."

That was just about all the money that the son possessed, but he remembered his vow, paid the money and took the casket home and placed it on the table that night when the Passover began. When he opened it, out sprang a frog.

The son's wife was sorely disappointed, but she fed the frog who ate everything in sight. The frog ate so much that by the end of the Passover, it had grown into an enormous monster. It kept growing and growing and soon required a special shed.

The son was profoundly puzzled. The frog was eating them out of house and home, but neither he nor his wife complained. They were willing to sell all that they had in order to feed the frog. Finally they reached a state of abject poverty. Then, and only then, did the son's wife lose faith and begin to cry.

To her astonishment, the frog monster spoke to her.

"You've treated me well. I will give you whatever you wish for."

"Give us food," sobbed the woman. Immediately there was a knock at the door and a huge basket of food was delivered.

Then the frog asked the son to request anything he wanted. The son reasoned, "A frog that speaks and performs wonders must be wise and learned, teach me wisdom."

The frog agreed, and his method of teaching was strange. He wrote out the Law and the seventy known languages of the world on strips of paper and ordered the son to swallow them. When he did this, the son became acquainted with everything, even the language of the beasts and the birds. Everyone regarded him as the most learned tzadik of his time.

One day the frog spoke again.

"The day has arrived when I must repay you for all the kindness you have shown me. Your reward shall be great. Come with me to the woods and you shall see marvels performed."

The son and his wife followed the giant frog to the woods very early one morning. When they arrived, the frog croaked, "Come to me all who live in the trees, caves and streams, and do what I tell you to do. Bring precious stones from the depths of the earth and roots and herbs."

The son and his wife looked in disbelief as hundreds of birds, thousands of insects, and all the animals in the woods, from the tiniest to the monsters, came and brought some gift to lay at the feet of the son and his wife who stood in total shock.

"All these belong to you," said the frog, pointing to the jewels. "And all of these herbs and the roots as well, because with them you will cure all diseases. I am rewarding you because you obeyed the wishes of the dying and did not question me."

The son thanked the frog and asked, "May we know who you are?"

The frog said, "I am the fairy son of Adam, gifted with the power of assuming any form. Farewell." With these words, the frog began to grow smaller and smaller until it was the size of an ordinary frog. Then it hopped into a stream and disappeared, and all the denizens of the woods returned to their haunts.

The son and his wife made their way home with their treasures. They became famous for their wealth, their wisdom, and their charity, and lived in happiness with all peoples for many years.

A giant frog on Route 66. Was this a sign? How could I not sign a contract with First Baptist Church of Willimantic?

Six months after I arrived, I was interviewed by the honorary mayor of Frog Town—the foremost frog on the lily pad—Wayne Norman, host of the longest running morning radio show in New England. We chatted on his show about the spiritual journey that brought me to Willimantic. I referred to being the only Jewish kid in Tilton School, Woodstock, Jews for Jesus, the yellow Corvette on Route 66, Zaydah and the giant frog on Route 66, and I talked about Hollywood Presbyterian Church. When Wayne heard me say Hollywood Presbyterian Church, his eyes became more rooted to the ground than a tree. He quickly took a break and excitedly called his mother in Hollywood: "Mom, you're not going to believe this but I'm interviewing Fred Shapiro, who used to go to our church Hollywood Pres." He put me on the phone and his mom didn't seem to care that we had gotten her out of bed at 5:00 a.m. in Hollywood. We chatted about the legacy of the church (especially the Hollywood Help Line) and wondered if we had met each other, perhaps passed the peace to each other during a Sunday service.

Wayne Norman and I have gotten to know each other a little bit better. I even have my own gospel music show on WILI. Whenever I go into the studio, I can't help think about Judy and the Hollywood Help Line. If any call ever changed my life, it was that one. When I do my Sunday morning and Sunday night gospel show, I hope only that the forty-year-old miracle is still manifested.

# CHAPTER 41

"Many people think that heroin is a big city, urban drug. It's not. It's in Willimantic. And it's infesting Willimantic. And it's a small town. Willimantic is a drug-infested small town, with a population of 15,000 – 16,000 people, in the middle of Connecticut. It's in the middle, some say, of nowhere – unless you want to buy or sell drugs."[87]

Fred Shapiro, a Jewish pastor in the documentary, makes a good point about Willimantic and comments that, "sometimes you have to learn to love the dandelions."[88]

When I arrived at First Baptist Church of Willimantic, I discovered that hookers used our parking lot to get business and our bushes to do business. Some members wanted to see the church close its doors, preferring a beautiful funeral rather than a messy rebirth.

A few months after I arrived, a film director from Philadelphia named Josh Goldbloom came to Willimantic to shoot a feature-length documentary that would refute Dan Rather's claim on 60 Minutes. I invited Josh to live with me while filming. As a result, he invited me to be prominently featured in the film. What an opportunity to promote First Baptist as a compassionate element of renewal and change.

---

[87] Dan Rather 60 Minutes
[88] Review of Heroin Town by Constantin Traian Preda . . . Orlando Fla

Josh promised that I'd have power to edit any scenes I appeared in that I felt jeopardized my role as a Baptist minister. The film was scheduled to have its premiere at Eastern Connecticut University.

Before the premier, Josh called and said that the scene that gets the loudest applause from preview audiences is a scene where I use strong profanity. When I expressed concern and reminded him of our agreement, he agreed to delete that scene from the Eastern Connecticut University premier. That night at Eastern University, the audience heard me swear. There was no loud applause, only the sound of two nuns sitting in back of me gasping. My date Carol hid her head.

As people left the auditorium, I was frozen to my seat. A woman walked over to me, took my hand, and said, "I wish my pastor had the courage to talk that way."

She came to church the following Sunday. Recently, a neighbor watched "Heroin Town" on Netflix. The film had not been edited, but I've learned to live with what I said, and somehow it doesn't sound so bad nine years later. The "Heroin Town" premiere was my third date with Carol. Our second date was the Fred Eaglesmith show.

# CHAPTER 42

*That God you got is a fancy God and he's not the one I know.*
*He don't live in parking lots outside of monster homes.*
*My God ain't in the government, He don't put on a big show.*
*That God you got is a fancy God and he's not the one I know.*[89]

The Willimantic Camp Meeting Association was established on September 3, 1860 and is one of the oldest, continuing religious camp meetings on the East coast. In the early days, up to 15,000 people would attend the weeklong camp meetings. Earlier, I referred to Reverend Charles Dorchester as one of four people who kept me from quitting seminary. I had never heard him preach and was excited to hear that he would be closing out the 2003 camp meeting season. I guess I didn't expect 15,000 people that night, but I sure expected more than fifty.

One of the fifty was Carol. Carol had once attended one of our worship celebrations at First Baptist. I had also seen her when I gave a concert at the campground, but we had never really talked. Reverend Dorchester and his wife Mary had been Carol's neighbor for years and loved her.

By the end of the night, he wanted to make sure that I got to know her. This was the last sermon that Reverend Dorchester ever preached. He and his wife Mary now own a blueberry farm in Maine.

---

[89] Fred Eaglesmith: Fancy God – Tinderbox

Carol's friends were fans of a Canadian singer–songwriter named Fred Eaglesmith. She described him as a country singer who was appealing to Phish[90] heads. Okay, I loved Phish but didn't care much for country music, so I did not expect much. He was amazing.

A few months later, Fred was playing at The Narrows, a nightclub in Fall River, Massachusetts. Carol and I invited my son to join us to see him. I didn't know that one of his favorite teachers had a poster of Fred in his office. Joe liked Fred that night, but we both hated the opening act and laughed pretty loud when Fred cussed out the musician for being "too f***inn long and boring." It had been a long time since Joe and I agreed on music. I felt like screaming "God bless Fred!"

Let me jump ahead a few years. I checked out his website to see when Fred would be in the area. He was scheduled to be in Philadelphia on February 23 and in North Hampton, Massachusetts on February 26, with no dates in between. It was then that I thought I heard the Lord's voice say, "Call Fred and ask if he'll do a benefit for the church meal program."

My Response was, "Lord, he swears in his concerts, and I don't think he's a Christian."

I thought I heard God say something like, "We have nothing to lose. Remember we survived 'Heroin Town.'"

I called and was surprised to hear his agent, Bill Passalagua, say, "So you've heard his new Gospel CD, huh?" I had no idea that Fred had recorded Tinderbox, which he calls "A gospel CD for people who aren't religious." Bill Passalagua told me he would talk to Fred and call me back. He called me the next day.

"Fred would love to do a benefit for the community meal program."

---

[90] Phish is an American rock band noted for their musical improvisation, extended jams and loyal fan base.
Phish's music blends elements of rock, jazz, funk, folk, bluegrass, reggae, country, blues, and barbershop quartet.

When I brought the offer before the church board, there was skepticism. "We have never done a secular show in our sanctuary." The church agreed with the stipulation that Traveler (my gospel band) would open for him. I shuddered when I remembered Fred's opening act in Fall River.

I called Bill Passalagua to confirm the benefit date. When I shared my nervousness about opening with Fred and being cussed out, he simply advised, "Just keep the set short and don't do any boring hippy folk music. Also when Fred gets there he will immediately want some secluded room. He will stay there until the show."

February 25th, Fred arrived at First Baptist Church Willimantic.

At 7:00 p.m., Traveler took the stage for a 20-minute set. It didn't sound all that good to me. As soon as I got off stage, Kori (Fred's drummer–merchandise person) called out, "Fred would like to see you right now!"

I followed her into the darkened room where he was sitting. I could hear the Godfather theme in my head. *Had Traveler played too long? Was the set that bad? I was nervous, I did not want to be cussed out in the sanctuary.*

"Mr. Eaglesmith, I hope everything is okay. I hope we didn't go on too long."

Fred motioned me to sit down. "What do you mean?" he asked.

"I was there at The Narrows when you cussed out the opening act."

"Yeah, but he was terrible. You guys are not just good, you're brilliant. I'd like you to play at my summer picnic in Aylmer, Ontario in August."

When Fred took the stage, he raved about Traveler adding, "The beautiful thing is they don't know how good they are."

Fred was great that night. His fans loved him. The church loved him. Willimantic loved him. When I got home, there was a message on my answering machine.

"Hey Fred, this is Fred. The band and I talked it over. We ripped up the check you gave us. That's just the way we want it."

Fred has been to Willimantic four times since then and has raised over $8,000 for our community meal programs. Traveler has been to the picnic twice. God bless Fred Eaglesmith. He is often in my thoughts and prayers.

# CHAPTER 43

*Blending Traditional and Transformational Worship, the First Baptist Church of Willimantic is a caring Christian community located on Main Street by history and by choice. We invite all people without distinction that together we might live our lives by this three-fold calling:*

1. *Love God and One another.*
2. *Discover God's unique call and purpose for our individual lives.*
3. *Participate in transforming Willimantic into a safe, healthy, and inspiring community.*[91]

When I arrived at First Baptist, there was a Thursday night food ministry in place. A few members of the church would haul a Red Ryder wagon full of sandwiches and drinks outside and offer them to hungry people on Main St.

One night when it was especially cold, Kathy Duchesne and I opened the doors and let folks inside. It wasn't long before another night was added (this one included live music and a short devotional message) and then another. As our meal program expanded, some longtime church members stopped tithing and our attendance dropped. It was okay to feed folks sandwiches and coffee on Main Street, but don't let them into

---

[91] From the Mission Statement of First Baptist Church of Willimantic viewable at www.fbcwillimantic.org

our church. Some even put chains around the sanctuary doors. The rest of the church reacted, chains came off, and some longtime members left.

As one woman left, she warned, "The church will not survive without our support."

I really thought she was right. I had been in Willimantic for just over a year and was already beginning to seek out other pastoral possibilities. Then it was time for our annual meeting. No one was anxious to hear the treasurer's report. Julie laughed and bragged, "We took in more money this year than last year."

Some people are still convinced that on the night before that meeting, God deposited a large check in our account. I don't know about that. I do know that nothing can stop a God who can part the Red Sea, send me a yellow Corvette, get me elected class president at a Nazarene College, sees me through two divorces, and allows me to share a stage with Fred Eaglesmith. God is good.

# CHAPTER 44

*What's the price of a pet canary? Some loose change, right? And God cares what happens to it even more than you do. He pays even greater attention to you, down to the last detail — even numbering the hairs on your head! So don't be intimidated by all this bully talk. You're worth more than a million canaries.*[92]

While playing at Fred Eaglesmith's 2011 picnic in Aylmer, Ontario, I took a serious fall that intensified damage to my arthritic knee. Immediately upon returning from Canada, I was scheduled for knee replacement surgery. A month before the surgery, I met Tavish.

My wife Carol is a collector of Scottie ornaments. She has Scottie creamers, doorstops, tablecloths, key chains, handbags, vintage postcards, candleholders, lunch boxes, kitchen towels, pillows, toys, etc., but she had never owned a live Scottish terrier.

One night I dreamt that we owned a Scottish terrier named Tavish. When I told Carol about my dream, there was a trace of a smile, but also a subterranean sense that this dog would be impractical.

The day after we returned from Aylmer, we received a call from Christine, a veterinarian who attends our church. She had been driving home when she saw a dog standing in the middle of the road. She told

---

[92] Matthew 10: 29-31 as paraphrased in The Message

us that it appeared he was begging for her to run him over. She got out of the car to pick him up and move him to the side of the road. His coat of fur was shaggy and spotty. He had cysts on his body, was seriously underweight, and had a dirty matted underbelly. It looked as if he had been abandoned for months.

She picked him up and decided to take him home with her. The following day she brought him to her office, shaved his fur, operated on him, and began nursing him back to health. During this time, she called the police and canvased every home in the neighborhood asking if anyone had lost a Scottish terrier.

Knowing how much Carol wanted a Scotty, she called us. We agreed to let him stay for a while and see how things worked out. A year and a half later, things are not only working out, but Tavish has proven to be one of the greatest examples of God's love for me than I could ever begin to imagine.

Recently we entertained a couple who thought they recognized Tavish. Because they live only two blocks away from the veterinarian who found him, this seems quite possible. They claimed that their neighbor used to own a Scottish terrier, and they were glad to not see the dog around much anymore.

When I asked why they were glad, Mrs. H. remembered, "The woman's son used to tie the dog to the back of his motorcycle and drag him along the street." As we looked at Tavish, weeping and glowing in appreciation of God's care and provision.

# CHAPTER 45

*"Anyone can carry his burden, however hard, until nightfall. Anyone can do his work, however hard, for one day. Anyone can live sweetly, patiently, lovingly, purely, till the sun goes down. And this is all life really means."*[93]

While recuperating from knee replacement surgery in the rehab center, Tavish came to visit me. I enjoyed his visit more than I enjoyed a call from my oncologist informing me that the blood work ordered by the surgeon who did my knee surgery revealed that my cancer had returned for the fifth time. As soon as I could walk again, I underwent treatments at the Dana-Farber Cancer Institute in Boston and at the Oncology Associates at Windham Hospital in Willimantic. I was in treatment until June 2012 and am now in remission. I don't think too much about the eight months of treatment. It is all overshadowed by events that happened between August and October of 2012.

In August, Carol and I planned to drive to Hershey, Pennsylvania to see Joyce Meyer and then drive to the Rock and Roll Hall of Fame and Museum in Cleveland. At the last minute, we cancelled the second part of the trip to Cleveland so that we could get back in time to celebrate a parishioner's 50th wedding anniversary. We boarded Tavish for a week at a local vet and took off.

---

[93]  Robert Louis Stevenson

Carol and I don't always travel well together. My driving gets her nervous, and driving through New York City, New Jersey, and Pennsylvania provided ample opportunities for Carol to be stressed about my speeding, passing other cars, speeding through yellow lights, making U-turns, and other poor driving habits. By the time we reached Hershey, I did not feel that we were in the sweetest place on earth, and I didn't want to see Joyce Meyer.

For the next two days, everything that could've possibly gone wrong did. In six years, I had never heard Carol speak about the devil hindering or opposing us until this trip.

At her meeting, Joyce Meyer seemed to address everything that Carol and I had been going through. At one point, she quoted Malachi 3: 10: from the Amplified Bible, *"Bring all the tithes (the whole tenth of your income) into the storehouse, that there may be food in My house, and prove Me now by it, says the Lord of hosts, if I will not open the windows of heaven for you and pour you out a blessing, that there shall not be room enough to receive it."*

We wept, agreeing to recommit our lives to Jesus and one other.

The ride home was a lot better, with both of us consciously aware not to be irritable. While driving home, I even heard God let me know that this would be the last chapter of this book. It felt good to know that the book had an ending and that it was an upbeat ending.

We picked up Tavish and drove home. Carol entered the house first and her shriek pierced my heart. There was water everywhere, along with collapsed walls and ceilings, and destroyed furniture. Our second floor water tank had exploded, and water had destroyed the interior of our home. It would be two to three months before our home was livable.

For the next three weeks, Carol, Tavish, and I stayed at three different hotels. The insurance company finally placed us in a rental home at 290 Lewiston Avenue. As we arrived, the very first person we saw was Kathy Duchesne who lived next door.

I was reminded of how Linda had shown up at God's Provision the very day that Wendy and I had moved there twenty-seven years earlier. We walked over to Kathy's house and Kathy mentioned that the house next door to hers was for sale. Later, the realtor handling the property we were staying in pointed at the very same house that Kathy had pointed to and said, "I can show it to you; it's a Victorian that needs a lot of work but it has a dry basement."

The next day, August 30, the reading in my *Smith Wigglesworth*[94] *Devotional* stated:

> *It is quite easy to construct a building if the foundation is secure. On the other hand, a building will be unstable if it does not have a solid understructure. Likewise, it is not very easy to rise spiritually unless we have a real spiritual power working within us. It will never do for us to be top heavy – the basement must always be firmly set.*

That day Carol and I did something that many would call crazy. We placed an offer on that house with the "firmly set basement" simply because we believed God called us to do it. We did not know where the money would come from! We did not know if the former house would sell. We simply obeyed the voice of God without a clue as to what would happen. After all, the very best moments in my life have been moments where I listened to God's voice without a clue as to what would happen.

On August 30, I did the right thing. I swallowed my fear for just one day. For just one day, I didn't grumble about my burdens. For just one day, I walked in faith and obedience. Robert Louis Stevenson reminds me that one day is enough.

---

[94] Smith Wigglesworth is considered by many to be the Father of modern Pentecostalism

# EPILOGUE

In chapter 34 I questioned whether my calling is governed by my religion or my obsession with acceptance and affirmation? Is it possible that I've learned from Hannah Dustin how to use my Bible as a tomahawk to kill sleeping Christians? Have I destroyed more churches than I have delivered?"

As a child, I regularly asked Zaydah, "What's the purpose of life?" His answer was always the same: "To achieve closeness to God."

"And, Zaydah, how do I achieve closeness to God?"

Zaydah would take my hand and say, "We draw close to God by doing mitzvah."[95] When I grumbled, "No one can do that many good deeds or live that close to God," he would remind me of Eliyahu HaNavi (Elijah the Prophet) who demonstrated so much devotion to God that he never died but ascended to the heavens in a chariot of fire.

During the Passover Seder, a cup of wine is set aside for Elijah. At the end of the Seder, the door is opened, and Elijah visits every Jewish home

---

[95] In its primary meaning mitzvah refers to one of the 613 commandments given by God to Moses at Mount Sinai and the seven Rabbinic commandments instituted later for a total of 620. In its secondary meaning, mitvah refers to any good deed or act of charity performed out of religious duty.

that is celebrating the Seder. Everyone at the Seder table stands and Elijah is welcomed into the household and is honored as the forerunner to the Messiah. The participants promise to live a more Godly life through performing mitzvahs so that Messiah may come next year.

On the last Passover I spent with Zaydah, I asked why there still hadn't been enough holiness and mitzvah so that Elijah would be satisfied and stick around to bring about the coming of Messiah. I didn't know it then, but zaydah's answer to me was the same answer the first Kabbalist Isaac ben Solomon Ashkenazi Luria gave to his protégé Rabbi Chaim Vital, *"In the time before the Messiah it will be so challenging to correctly observe mitzvah that the mitzvah done in those times will have more power than they did in the earlier times. Even though those mitzvahs may not be done as completely, but because they will be so difficult they will have the power to bring the Messiah."*[96]

Dr. Steve Ott had told me that it would be hard for me to change habits and stop running, but on the day that I decide to stop, I will find a new power to let people know about Jesus. I'm not sure that I'm telling more people about Jesus, but I know I'm doing more mitzvahs. I've been in Willimantic ten years and I haven't run. I didn't flee a flooded home. I didn't hightail it after the Heroin Town humiliation. I didn't leave when some longtime members left. Others ran, and I remained. I'm learning not to run so quickly from plagues. Perhaps it's because I pastor in a city known as "Frog City." Most people have no idea what the giant frogs symbolize. The answer is maybe the most fantastic story I've attempted to tell in this book.

As France and England laid claim to American territory, Willimantic had experienced the darkest period of its history. There had been so much bloodshed and carnage, and so many children had died that citizens trembled at the prospects of "judgments of God."

In June 1754, people were roused from their sleep by a mysterious, loud noise. As the sound became more deafening, many fell to their knees

---

[96] Tractate Avot 4:1

terrified that this was the "Day of Judgment." Others grabbed guns to fend off the invaders. Town historians write that it was bedlam. People were firing guns at each other while begging God for forgiveness. The chaos continued all night. The light of dawn revealed the truth. Thousands of dead frogs were seen everywhere. A severe drought caused the last ponds to dry up and the green bullies were desperately seeking the last bits of water and fighting each other in a turf battle. Ellen D Larned described the citizens' response in The History of Windham County:

> *"Some were well pleased, and some were mad;*
> *Some turned it off with laughter;*
> *And some would never hear a word*
> *About the thing, thereafter.*
> *Some vowed that if the Devil, himself,*
> *Should come, they would not flee him,*
> *And if a frog they ever met,*
> *Pretended not to see him."*[97]

Compellingly enough, dream analysts advocate that to dream of frogs in low marshy places foretells trouble, but there's also the promise that the trouble will be overcome by the kindness of others. How can frogs in any way be connected to kindness? If you asked Zaydah he'd shut off the Western he was watching on TV and tell you the frog story that I told earlier.

Recently a monster awoke the Willimantic community. Two homeless men were brutally beaten and left for dead as they slept on a bench in a garden park adjacent to the Frog Bridge. Both of these men were regular guests at the First Baptist Community Meals; both of these men were my friends. Today both men are well largely due to the kindness of others in our community.

---

[97] The History of Windham County, Connecticut, Volume I" pp 560-563; by Ellen D. Larned

As over 100 of us gathered at the Garden on the Bridge to show support for the two men who were beaten, people sang their songs and shared their stories. At one point, I was able to remind one of the victims of pieces of my story. He had already heard some of these pieces before. He had heard about the ten-year-old boy in the museum who knew how many states were in the Union during the Civil War. He had heard about the poor and frightened college dropout who had the opportunity to go to seminary. He had heard about my five bouts with cancer. And he knows that I am utterly convinced that the lowest and darkest moments when I believe God to do impossible things are the greatest, brightest moments in my life.

The day I am offering to you is almost sixty-three years long. During the course of this day, there has been abandonment, beatings, voluminous mistakes, and muddles. But because the foundation is firmly set by my suffering and adversity, the day is filled with inordinate, boundless joy.

For your tomorrow, I give you my today."

CPSIA information can be obtained at www.ICGtesting.com
Printed in the USA
BVOW03s1343311213

340484BV00004B/5/P